PRAISE FOR *AI FOR LAWYERS*

AI for Lawyers pulls together a series of easy-to-read vignettes that cut through the mystique, noise and bullshit surrounding AI for legal. It provides excellent guidance for lawyers who don't know which way to travel when they finally arrive at the intersection of legal services and technology—which is most of the profession!

—Mitchell Kowalski, author of
The Great Legal Reformation: Notes from the Field

Noah Waisberg and Dr. Alexander Hudek have taken a complex topic and made it accessible and enjoyable. Like it or not, artificial intelligence and machine learning, particularly when combined with 5G connectivity, computing on the edge of networks and eventually quantum computing, will advance by leaps and bounds to automate and change the way we practice law. It is also leveling the playing field between lawyers practicing in big firms vs. small firms. Wherever, whatever and however you are currently practicing, *AI for Lawyers* will open your eyes and make you feel excited and empowered to be part of the future.

—Louis Lehot, founder,
L2 Counsel, P.C.

Alex and Noah have written a demystifying AI book which will help lawyers take advantage of AI technology to create new customer value. They cover the key resources and processes needed to deliver value, which will help all lawyers capture this AI-driven value in their go-to-market approaches, enabling them to develop new ways to solve old problems.

—Michelle Mahoney, Executive Director,
Innovation, King & Wood Mallesons

There is little doubt that the legal industry has experienced a cataclysmic extinction moment, where yesterday's ways of working are tomorrow's fossilised memories. The changing expectations of both the consumers of legal services, and the next generations of lawyers, has seen to it that the practice of law has been changed forever by the arrival of advanced technologies.

In *AI for Lawyers*, Noah and Alex have created the definitive guide on the role of technology in the legal industry. No two authors are better qualified to commentate on how our world is changing. This is a must-read for anyone in the industry and those planning on living a life within the law.

—Justin North, Managing Director,
Morae Global Corporation

The intersection of science fiction and lawyering is both a terrible idea for a movie and a very real problem for attorneys. The terror that artificial intelligence will replace human lawyers and spew steam from the keyboard while trying to define "love" during an ill-fated document review terrifies some folks. And that's unfortunate because when stripped of its sci-fi mystique, "artificial intelligence" here in the real world is both non-frightening and entirely essential to a thriving 21st century law practice. Waisberg and Hudek's book provides lawyers a friendly, brass tacks introduction to this oft-misunderstood technology and provides straightforward examples of how AI can advance your practice . . . and, sometimes, how it's already advanced your practice without you even knowing it.

—**Joe Patrice, Senior Editor, Above the Law**

Although many lawyers have strong views on the use of AI in the law, very few in fact have a solid grasp of the potential and limitations of this technology. Worse, some lawyers even have the temerity to use 'AI' as a verb, claiming—almost arbitrarily—that 'you can AI' this or that legal task. Into this world of bold confusion and brazen conjecture, I therefore extend a heartfelt welcome to *AI for Lawyers*. This book brings the clarity, deep technical expertise, practical experience, and commercial insight that are sorely needed in the field.

—**Richard Susskind, author of *Tomorrow's Lawyers* (2017),**
***The Future of the Professions* (2015), *The End of Lawyers* (2008), and**
***Expert Systems in Law* (1987)**

Noah and Alex clearly show that the use of AI-embedded software in the legal world will soon be as ubiquitous as the use of word processing. The authors (a Who's Who of experts in legal technology) cover an extraordinarily broad range of AI-software types and applications—from machine learning to expert systems. The book is an essential read for solo practitioners all the way up to those practicing in the lofty heights of the elite firms around the world and for the technology gurus who enable them. To succeed in law in the coming years, you will need to use AI. To be prepared to use AI, reading this book is a must.

—**Harris Tilevitz, Chief Technology Officer, Skadden**

I loved this book! AI is increasingly becoming a driver of success for high performing lawyers and law firms. This book is a quick, easy introduction to it. Every lawyer should read it.

—**Kent Zimmermann, strategic advisor to law firms**

AI FOR LAWYERS

NOAH WAISBERG AND DR. ALEXANDER HUDEK

AI FOR LAWYERS

HOW ARTIFICIAL INTELLIGENCE IS ADDING VALUE, AMPLIFYING EXPERTISE, AND TRANSFORMING CAREERS

WILEY

Published by John Wiley & Sons, Inc., Hoboken, New Jersey.
Published simultaneously in Canada.

For general information on our other products and services or for technical support,
please contact our Customer Care Department within the United States at (800)
762-2974, outside the United States at (317) 572-3993 or fax (317) 572-4002.

Wiley publishes in a variety of print and electronic formats and by print-on-demand.
Some material included with standard print versions of this book may not be included
in e-books or in print-on-demand. If this book refers to media such as a CD or DVD
that is not included in the version you purchased, you may download this material
at http://booksupport.wiley.com. For more information about Wiley products, visit
www.wiley.com.

Library of Congress Cataloging-in-Publication Data is Available:
ISBN 9781119723844 (Hardcover)
ISBN 9781119723899 (ePDF)
ISBN 9781119723882 (ePub)

Cover Design: Wiley
Cover Image: © Edo Cuallo
Author Photos: © Joanne Son

SKY10023332_121720

To those driving law practice forward.

Contents

Part III   The Plan: Leverage data
and AI to expand and future
proof your practice   **153**

Introduction

Lorie Waisberg kept checking his watch as he waited for the typist to finish the document. She was making the standard three copies using whitener and two pieces of carbon paper. He was anxious because he knew that getting extra copies would take time. When she handed the pages off to Lorie, he took off out the doors of his dad's law firm and down three flights of stairs, across the street, and continued his pace for two blocks, dodging traffic as he made his way to Sudbury's City Hall. They had one of the only copy machines in town, and the Waisbergs could use it in emergencies. Lorie had two concerns as he ran: one was that city hall closed at 4:00 p.m. promptly. The other was that he might not be able to find the person who held the only key to the copier room.

As Lorie made his way into the building, he saw that the clock in the lobby was closing in on 4:00 p.m. He found Gary, the chief engineer, better known to many as "the guy with the copier room key." Gary was grabbing his jacket to head out for the day.

"Gary, it's just three copies, please," panted Lorie. Gary smiled. "Okay, just for you," and, with that, he unlocked the copier room.

It was 1959, and technology was a far cry from where it is today. Yet it was the year that US President Dwight Eisenhower first sent a message to Canadian Prime Minister John Diefenbaker by means of a radio signal bouncing off the moon as a forerunner of modern satellite communications. Such long-range communication would be one of many new technologies that Lorie Waisberg would see during this long legal career. After starting at what was then known as Goodman & Goodman (a small firm at the time, and today one of Canada's leading firms), he witnessed a parade of new technology, from the popular IBM Selectric typewriters to the new correctable models that made errors fixable. In the early 1970s, the Lexis service was introduced, which allowed lawyers to search case law on computers rather than laboriously poring through books. Fax machines became widely used in the early 1980s, spitting documents out at one to two pages printed per minute. This was a big improvement on waiting for couriered documents, especially when working with others far away. Shortly thereafter, word processors replaced typewriters. Then Lorie got a computer on his desk, then got the internet. "People didn't trust email at first; they wondered who else could see it," recalls Lorie. Eventually, email became a preferred means of communication. Lorie got a BlackBerry.

There were large technology changes over my dad's career, a lawyer for more than 30 years. His father, Harry, a lawyer and then a judge, started his legal career in the mid-1930s and saw new technology and other changes over his many years in law practice.

When I became a lawyer in 2006, email, the internet, and electronic legal research were standard, but we still regularly used physical books to look up information. "The printers" was an actual physical place. And, while virtual data rooms were popular, I had pleasant in-person due diligence trips to St. Louis and Pittsburgh. ("Pleasant" because the host company inevitably shut its doors at some civilized hour, as opposed to my New York Biglaw firm.) As a corporate lawyer, I had little to no specialized technology. We used email, Word (souped-up with some fancy toolbars), Excel, and PowerPoint (rarely!), the internet, virtual data rooms, and document comparison software. Someone passed around a link to an online version of the securities "Redbook," but we mostly used the hefty physical version, and we (or our assistants) would diligently insert update pages into it as they arrived. If you asked, you could get Acrobat Professional. And, with some real effort and a partner's permission, the firm would even give you a second computer monitor and, maybe, a laptop. VoIP phones were apparently coming soon, meaning we could take calls from home and have no one be the wiser. We could remotely access our work computer via Citrix. I really appreciated my fancy telephone headset. Things are different now.

Obviously, the legal profession has advanced quite a bit since my grandfather and father's days as lawyers, and even since mine. Yet, challenges remain part of the job. I recall having to push hard as I started my law career, sifting through what seemed like endless pages of contracts, balancing multiple deals running simultaneously, and worrying that more work was coming when I saw my BlackBerry's light flashing red. I recall working an all-nighter and sending a draft out just after 6 a.m.; almost immediately I received comments back from a hedge fund client who had gotten to his desk early.

Despite the ongoing changes in legal technology, widespread misconceptions remain that (i) lawyers are loath to adopt new technology, and (ii) technology has historically not been a major factor in law. Yet lawyers have regularly adopted new technology at near-ubiquitous levels, and technology has played a key role in changing how law is practiced. For years, technology has made many lawyer tasks easier to complete, raising the performance bar and allowing lawyers to focus more attention on the needs of their clients. Today, artificial intelligence is the latest step in driving the practice of law forward. AI is getting heavily used in law. It offers real advantages for lawyers who embrace it, and perils for those who don't. I'm happy to be a part of this change, and, just for the record, my dad is happy for me.

—*Noah Waisberg*

The Evolution of Kira

Noah Waisberg and Dr. Alexander Hudek first got together in January 2011, introduced by a friend-of-a-friend. At the time, Noah had recently quit his job as an M&A lawyer at Weil, Gotshal & Manges, a very large New York City firm. Alex had recently gotten a Computer Science PhD from the University of Waterloo. Alex was doing post-doctoral research at the time.

For years before leaving Weil, Noah wrestled with the inefficiencies he (and friends at other firms) struggled with. Junior corporate lawyers spent vast amounts of time doing work they hated, weren't very good at, and clients hated paying for. All at—back then—over $300/hour. It seemed unsustainable. And perhaps an opportunity. Noah thought, "What are things junior corporate lawyers spend a lot of time on? Can they be done better?" He played with several ideas, but they didn't seem like they would make great businesses. Then, in conversation with his wife one crisp November day, he started to think about contracts. He realized three things:

1. People spend a ton of time reviewing contracts.

2. They make lots of mistakes in this work, even when they are top graduates, from top schools, who have been through extensive training.

3. People often review contracts for the same things over and over. In M&A, it can be change of control, assignment, exclusivity, and the like. In securities, maybe it's restricted payments baskets or asset sale covenants. In real estate, it might be base and additional rent, subletting, or maintenance responsibilities. And so on.

Since people looked through contracts for the same things over and over, Noah thought it might be possible to build software to help lawyers find and extract this information. He needed a technical partner, and teamed up with Alex to solve the problem. Based on talking with Alex and other Waterloo computer science PhD grads, they thought it would take them four months to harness available machine learning and apply it to this problem. They thought it might take them six months to raise money to pursue their idea, and decided to just plow forward; they could raise money later.

After six months, the software was not working properly—it just wasn't accurate—and there was little chance it would improve anytime soon. As Alex learned more, he realized the state of the art technology didn't work well on their problem. They faced scientific uncertainty. They might crack the problem in three months, but it could take up to 10 years. At that point, they certainly didn't think they could raise any money. Telling a venture capitalist that they thought they would lick the problem in a decade didn't seem like it would make a very compelling pitch, especially when the end product would make lawyers faster at their work.

They Just Kept Building

By 2013, two-and-a-half years later, the software was finally accurate. Early customers found they could do contract review in 20% to 90% less time, with the same, or greater, accuracy.

Sales were *slooooooow*; few people were paying to use the software. Two-and-a-half years of operations, a hard technical problem solved, but little revenue to show for it, selling to lawyers (who were reputed to be anti-tech and anti-efficiency) seemed like a hard VC pitch. So they stayed focused on improving the product and getting people to pay to use it. By 2014, there was more interest in the software, and Alex built a crude version of a long-desired feature that allowed users themselves to teach the software to find new concepts. Now, a person could teach the system without feeling the need for a technical expert at their side. This was huge. Clients could highlight and tag provisions in a document, press a button, and it would learn what to look for. This, plus a market that was getting more and more focused on efficient legal work, ignited the sales of Kira. The company grew from 4 to 8 people in 2014, up to some 35 in 2016, as the customer base also grew. In summer 2018, bootstrapped Kira Systems reached 100 team members and took its first outside funding. As we write this Introduction in summer 2020, there are 240 Kirans.

A healthy majority of the world's biggest and best law firms subscribe to Kira's AI contract analysis software, including 19 of the top 25 M&A firms, 7 of the "Vault 10" most prestigious US law firms, 11 of the UK's top 12 firms by revenue, 5 of Canada's "Seven Sisters," and leading firms in countries including Brazil, Denmark, Germany, India, Norway, and Portugal. It's not just giant firms using Kira. Law firms ranging from solos and smalls to several of the top few firms in places like Missouri or Tennessee subscribe, too. So do most Big Four firms, sometimes for their lawyers, but also for thousands of accountants or consultants to use. Plus, a growing number of corporates, which sometimes use the software to help in-house lawyers, but they often deploy it to help them understand what their contracts say to help with business problems or to augment contract management systems.

Why Are Noah and Alex Worth Reading on the Use of AI in the Legal Industry?

Why are we well qualified to be a guide through this industry? In some ways, we're not. We run a legal AI software company and so may be biased. On the plus side, we have been working on legal AI for almost a decade, meaning we're among the longest-active people in the industry. We have built among the most successful businesses in legal AI. And we bring individual advantages to the table, too. Noah has practiced law, giving him empathy for what it's like to be an attorney. Alex has deep technical knowledge. He began programming computers at age 8, and since has worked on the human genome project, gotten his PhD in computer science, and worked heavily with machine learning on text, as well as formal logics.

In the Pages Ahead

We hope you will come away from this book with two learnings:

1. AI is here in law practice, like it or not. It is already in heavy use in parts of the legal industry, and this will only grow. In time, its use will be ubiquitous.
2. AI can be great for lawyers, if they let it. It can help them do more, better work, generating happier clients; give them more interesting and fulfilling careers; and help them make more money.

This book is not intended to be an exhaustive review of everything happening in legal AI. We are not going to tell you about all areas where AI is being used in law, or which vendors are best. Honestly, it's changing quickly, and we hope this book will be helpful for years into the future. But there's a deeper reason we wrote this book. We believe that if you come away believing that AI can help your legal career, you'll be able to take the next steps to figure out how. Think of it as more like *A Year in Provence* or *Paris to the Moon* than the *Michelin Guide*. More *The Old Patagonia Express* or *In Patagonia* than the *Footprint South America Handbook*. We aren't going to tell you where to get the best socca in Nice, or where to stay in Ushuaia. But, hopefully, we will inspire you to go. Of course, this book is about legal AI, not France, and we're no Paul Theroux or Bruce Chatwin when it comes to writing. Nevertheless, we are optimistic you will find this book worth spending your valuable time with.

Among the many specific points addressed, *AI for Lawyers* will focus on:

- Why AI is now so vital in the legal workspace and how you can expand your opportunities through AI and technology.
- How to amplify legal knowledge through the use of AI.
- The various types of AI tools available including eDiscovery, legal research, contract analysis software, expert systems, and litigation analytics.
- How to incorporate AI into large, mid-sized, or small practices.

While Noah and Alex are among the most knowledgeable people in the world on contract analysis software and why lawyers should embrace AI, others know more than they do about some areas under the legal AI umbrella. So, along with the expertise of the authors, you will also find significant contributions by leading industry experts on some topics. This includes Carolyn Elefant on AI for solo and small-firm lawyers; Mary O'Carroll, Jason Barnwell, and Corinne Geller on modern legal jobs; Dera Nevin on AI in eDiscovery; Jake Heller, Laura Safdie, and Pablo Arredondo on AI in legal research; Joshua Walker and Anthony Niblett on litigation analytics; Amy Monaghan and Alicia Ryan supplementing Alex and Noah on contract analysis; and the magisterial Michael Mills on expert systems. Their background, experience, and insights add to the book's depth.

You needn't read this book chapter by chapter. Some chapters may be relevant for you in your practice, others not. Chapters 1, 2, and 5 are more general interest, primarily focused on objections to and opportunities from adopting AI. Chapter 4 focuses on how AI is creating new types of legal jobs. Chapter 6 discusses ethical issues around legal AI. Chapter 3 should be interesting for solo and small-firm lawyers, but not as useful for Biglaw or in-house readers. Part II (Chapters 7–11) focus on specific areas where AI has caught on in law practice. If you're a corporate or tax lawyer, Chapter 10 (contract analysis software) and Chapter 11 (expert systems) should be most relevant for you. If you're a litigator, Chapter 7 (eDiscovery), Chapter 8 (legal research), and Chapter 9 (litigation analytics) will be more interesting. Part III (Chapter 12) focuses on adopting AI into practice. The Conclusion is more general audience.

This book includes many quotes from people we think have something to add. Unless the source is attributed in an endnote, these quotes come from correspondence with the authors.

AI is here to stay and is changing how lawyers work. It can significantly benefit your career. If you're not already onboard, the time is now. *AI for Lawyers* can position you to get front and center in this new era of law practice. Let's go!

AI FOR
LAWYERS

PART I

The Point

AI in law is here to stay. It's time to take advantage

CHAPTER 1

How Lawyers Learned to Stop Worrying and Love AI

S imon G. is a 46-year-old corporate partner in a major New York–based law firm. He had been a partner for nearly 10 years when he took over as the relationship lead with one of the firm's top clients, a prominent Fortune 500 corporation.

This client was a major source of revenue for Simon's firm and several others. For many years, the firm was on the client's "panel" of legal service providers. To do any legal work for this company, you had to be on its panel. Each firm on the panel was designated for specific types of engagements and projects, and each would form its own deals with the client.

Everyone at the firm who worked on this client's "team" knew in-house lawyers and executives there very well. They had longstanding bonds formed over weeks-upon-weeks cooped up in conference rooms working on deals, as well as dinners, drinks, Yankee games, theater nights, parties, and more. The families of the partners and those of the corporate executives also got to know each other and would be invited to weddings and other family events. One senior partner at the firm even bought a summer house to be near a bunch of executives from this client.

Every three years, the client would go through the process of reselecting its panel of law firms to represent the firm. During each selection process over the decade in which Simon had been a corporate partner, the process had proceeded seamlessly, without even a hiccup.

Now, several of the firm's senior partners were beginning to transition into retirement. Simon was in a position to take on the leadership role of this major client relationship. This was everything he had worked toward. But, as he prepared to take over the leadership role, he quickly found himself in a major predicament.

This time, something was very different in the panel selection process. Instead of Simon's firm and other top-tier firms offering their typical 10–20% discounts, several top-notch firms, including a few that had never served on the panel before, were offering crazy discounts, some as much as 50% below their normal rates. Simon knew that these were excellent firms; he couldn't knock their quality, and he couldn't understand how they could afford to offer such low rates. Worse, he knew his firm could not afford to compete against these offers. Simon's heart sank. He realized that despite decades of great work and strong relationship development by Simon and his mentors, it was painfully clear that the firm was going to be priced out of working with this important client.

Shocked by how the panel selection was going, Simon immediately got on his computer and started doing what he should have done years prior to the panel review—discovering how law practice was changing, rather than assuming the longstanding relationship with this client would simply continue uninterrupted.

Simon spent hours over the next several days studying the competitive landscape, learning about what he and the retiring senior partners had missed. They had overlooked a very important aspect of today's legal industry: the greater drive for efficient work. Now Simon would have to figure out how to make up for falling so far behind his competitors. What he learned was that his competitors, thanks to innovations like AI, were able to do better work in less time. Through tracking and analyzing the time spent to do tasks as well as realization rates, Simon's competitors could figure out how to offer lower unit prices and still make money. Simon's firm was plenty sophisticated when it came to their legal skills, but, Simon was coming to realize, they were seriously outgunned when it came to the modern practice of law. To remain competitive, Simon and his firm would have to embrace technology in a big way to win over major clients and potentially impress their (now former) biggest client in three years at the next panel review.

Simon's problem was not uncommon, and not unique to Biglaw.

If you're a solo estate planning lawyer, how do you compete with online legal solutions like LegalZoom, who offer a will for $179?

If you're a small firm litigator, how do you compete with a bigger firm that has access to case data that's not as easy for you to obtain?

If you have a high-volume practice, how do you compete with firms that spend less time on customer intake because they use software that shortens the intake process and provides clients with self-help?

Now the question for Simon and his law firm was, could they do it? Could they get back in good favor with their most prestigious client?

AI has been a godsend for countless young law firm associates who once toiled late into the night to gather and review data, but has it played a more significant role across law practice? Let's find out. Before launching into the pros and cons of AI and the resistance and opportunities we have encountered, let's explain our definition of AI.

What Is AI?

For the purposes of this book, we consider AI to be any task a computer does that shows "human-like" intelligence or better. The precise edges of this definition are less important to us than the overall impact that AI and similar technologies have on society and the practice of law. To illustrate, let's talk about a few prominent types of AI tasks and techniques.

The field of AI encompasses many subdisciplines, including machine learning, expert systems, and other reasoning technology. At different points in history, a particular technique might be the face of AI. Although expert systems were once all the rage, today deep learning (a type of machine learning) is extremely popular.

In fact, not too long ago, arithmetic was considered an intelligent activity that only humans could perform. The term *computer* originally referred to people who did arithmetic and other math, not a machine that runs software (see Figure 1.1).

We wouldn't consider arithmetic to be artificial intelligence today, but 70 years ago, seeing a machine do this was magic. This shows how the definition of AI has a tendency to change over time. As tasks that we once considered untouchable by computers become routine, our definition of "human-like"

FIGURE 1.1   Early "computers" at work: Dryden Flight Research Center Facilities.
Source: From the Dryden Flight Research Center Photo Collection

intelligence becomes narrower. It's no longer news that computers can dominate at games of chess, and many people today take it for granted that they can speak to their phones. Self-driving cars exist and might become equally ordinary in the years to come.

AI can replicate certain aspects of human intelligence, such as pattern matching or categorization, and can often do such tasks much faster and more accurately than humans. However, AI doesn't have motivation and emotion like a human, and is generally not able to do things it wasn't designed to. The notion of a rogue AI is pervasive in popular culture and movies, but the reality is much less frightening. The AI that can learn languages is different from the AI that can hit a tennis ball, and there is no general connection between abilities. You can't assume that just because AI can win at *Jeopardy*, it will, therefore, make an amazing courtroom advocate. Those are different things. Doing one thing well doesn't mean it can do the other. Although we tend to promote the idea of AI having human intelligence by giving it human names such as Siri, Alexa, or Hal, it's still unable to emulate most of the human thought process, for better and for worse.

All that said, AI is able to do many remarkable things, such as understanding human speech, articulating responses, even writing passable text! How does it do this? It uses expert systems, machine learning, and constantly emerging innovation.

First let's talk about expert systems. These are computer systems that emulate the decision-making process of a human expert by asking a cascading series of questions. For example, an expert system might mimic what your doctor would do when they're making a diagnosis. It may ask: Do you have a fever? Do you have headaches? Do you feel dizziness? And so forth, then propose a diagnosis based on the answers you provided. The questions and decision trees in these systems must be handcrafted by human experts, generally falling into the "rule based" or "reasoning" subfield of AI. Expert systems are a good tool for a variety of tasks, but in many areas they are being replaced by machine learning.

Most of the AI you see in the news today is based on machine learning, including all the various deep-learning advances. Machine learning techniques allow computers to learn to perform tasks simply by observing data provided to them. It doesn't need experts to manually write complex rules, though it still does need to observe people to learn from them. Although the origins of machine learning are as old as those of expert systems, machine learning techniques didn't become widely effective until computers became more powerful. These systems excel at modeling unpredictable and complex tasks and can learn at a rate and scale far beyond what humans manually encoding knowledge in rules could achieve.

From driving a car, to serving as personal assistants, to face recognition, to web translation, to recommending a comedy you might like on Netflix, various types of AI are part of our world in big and small ways. In this book, the technology we discuss falls under our definition of AI. Others may have slightly different definitions of what "AI" is, but we would rather talk about its impact in law practice than debate the exact boundaries of the terms.

In the legal world, AI is being used for contract drafting, negotiation, and review; litigation document review and analysis; predicting case outcomes; suggesting courses of action; organizing legal research; time keeping; and lots more. It is opening up possibilities never before imagined and allowing lawyers to spend more time on law and less time on repetitive activities. AI is partnering with lawyers, rather than replacing them.

Appropriate Skepticism

Most people are averse to change, and lawyers are often perceived as being more change-averse than average. In fact, Dr. Larry Richard (a psychologist focused on lawyer behavior) has found that "skepticism" is consistently the highest-scoring personality trait among lawyers. According to Richard, lawyers have an average skepticism score around the ninetieth percentile, meaning they tend to be skeptical, even cynical, judgmental, argumentative, and self-protective. The general public tends to be at the fiftieth percentile on this trait, which means they'll be generally accepting of others, more trusting, and often give others the benefit of the doubt. Being skeptical is not necessarily a bad attribute for an attorney; helping clients mitigate risk is often a big part of the job. Therefore, it's especially understandable that lawyers have concerns when new technology lands on their doorstep.

"Why should we tamper with success? We've done it that way for 50 years and look where we are today." While a senior partner making that statement is not wrong, they miss that—despite many things staying the same—a lot has changed in the practice of law over the years. Change is inevitable, and today, technology is leading that change. It's no longer a matter of choice but a necessity for those who care to stay relevant.

While lawyers may be skeptical, history illustrates that when it comes to adopting, and even embracing, technology, the legal profession has often overcome initial reluctance and aggressively jumped on board.

For example, the 1970s saw the influx of computer technology. Law firms were able to use the Lexis UBIQ terminal, which later allowed lawyers to search case law online. This opened the door to numerous advances in the union between law and computer technology. Steve Carlotti, an eminent Rhode Island corporate lawyer, tells of their experience at Hinckley, Allen & Snyder LLP with early computer adoption: "We installed our first computer to handle time recording, billing, and accounting in 1976. Since then, profits per partner have risen more than 1200%, at least part of which is due to the ever-increasing use of computers and related software to deliver client services."

By the 1990s, eDiscovery had emerged with litigation support and court-room management software. This made it possible for legal professionals to quickly process, review, and produce electronic documents for research and to use for cases. It simply would not be possible to manage the discovery process of a large litigation—like the Microsoft antitrust case—without it. More recent examples of near-ubiquitous technology adopted by law firms over the past few decades have include PCs, laptops, email, BlackBerrys, document comparison software (aka redlining / blacklining / DeltaView), and virtual data rooms.

AI is just the latest in an ongoing succession of technological advances that have gained acceptance and approval by legal practitioners. However, like technical innovations that have come before, AI needed to meet industry standards, and it's a high "bar," so to speak.

Common Lawyer Objections to AI

In the course of pitching our own legal technology, we have had a lot of conversations with lawyers about using AI in their practice (so much so that Noah eventually wrote a children's book explaining machine learning in 256 rhyming words). While many lawyers have been enthusiastic or curious, lots had questions and reservations. Over the years, we've seen the same objections recur. Some are issues specific to our software. Many are more general, and could come up almost irrespective of the legal AI software in question.

Recurring issues we've found lawyers raise regarding AI are:

- "How can I trust AI software?"
- "What if our associates use the tech to 'cheat'?"
- "How are new lawyers going to grow into great lawyers with technology doing their work?"
- "Will using AI software impact (i) my duty to keep client information confidential, or (ii) lawyer–client privilege?"
- "Do I have to invest a lot of time in training AI to get value out of it?"
- "If AI makes lawyers way more efficient, will we need fewer lawyers?"
- "How does being more efficient work out for me if I bill hourly?"
- "How do I justify the extra expense of the software?"

"How Can I Trust AI Software?"

Back in 2014, an elite law firm partner explained his trust issue to us this way, and it stuck with us:

> *A couple of people at his firm had been sued for something that went wrong on a deal more than ten years ago. They spent over a decade fighting this lawsuit. His perspective was, "I know the manual way that I do it right now. I did it that way when I was a junior. I know the people who do the work too: I helped hire them, and I've trained them. I know how they work, and that they work hard. Even if it's not perfect, I know it and I know them. I trust them, knowing that my house and my professional career are on the line. How can I trust this new way of doing things?"*

Some find they can get to trust through seeing performance data. They run a test comparing their lawyers doing work the traditional way to those using the software, and see what the results are.

A TEST IN TRUST

By Meredith Williams-Range, Chief Knowledge and Client Value Officer at Shearman & Sterling LLP

I don't trust people in general; as a lawyer, I'm trained not to. If I don't trust people, then I won't trust technology. How do you overcome that sentiment among young lawyers to get them to adopt new technology? Well, you have to take a journey with them. You have to educate them, and you have to bring them along gradually in an effort that should result in them working the way you need them to work.

My experience is that lawyers often start from skepticism with technology, AI or not. So you should recognize that going into any conversation with a lawyer, it will be psychological. It's not about the piece of technology that you're trying to get them to use, it's simply trying to overcome the psychological burden within that individual, on an innate level. What we try to do at Shearman & Sterling is build trust through sponsorship. We have three critical business units: Disputes, Finance, and Corporate. If we're going to go down the path of bringing in a piece of AI, we have to build trust within those groups.

One of the things that we have adopted at the firm is what we call a proof of value, or POV. Why not a proof of concept (POC)? Well, POCs are great, because they prove that a piece of technology actually works. But working is table stakes. To us, the real questions are does it bring value to the partner or associate who will use it? Does it bring value to the client? At Shearman & Sterling, we run extensive POV programs. We measure—side-by-side with the status quo way of doing the task—whether the technology drives value. These tests generate numbers and data, and the results drive trust.

When we evaluated Kira, the POV ran for a full year. Our M&A teams used Kira to perform due diligence with past and live deals. Capital Markets teams tested it as a better way to capture data points. We did the same thing with many of our corporate teams. Different use cases, different purposes, but running the AI hand-in-hand with the young lawyer who was actually using it. Our administrative teams tried it, too. They were looking to review our heap of outside counsel guidelines and to understand some of our own contractual obligations.

When it comes to trust, one of the biggest objections you'll hear from partners is, "Well, how accurate is it?" Our response, after our POV, became, "How accurate are the associates and technology separate, but, also, how accurate are they combined?"

These can be hard questions to answer, but when we run our side-by-side POVs, we find there's more likelihood of human error than there is of AI error. When human and machine hold hands together, we found we did even better than either alone. The combination got us close to 100% accuracy. This is what our testing proved. That helped us create trust. Though this process was more data-heavy, it is pretty similar to how partners come to trust a new-to-practice associate. They see them in action, hear reports from others, and eventually come to trust them (or not).

In law, as well as in other industries, building trust is not an easy process. With over 200 partners, getting buy-in for an AI solution can sometimes feel like trying to get a piece of legislation through the House and Senate. But this is where having a practice like a POV enables you to win over partners quickly. The POV can demonstrate exactly how it's going to alleviate some of the burdens that you have that you're not being paid for. In my experience, that's a good way to build trust.

In the earlier days of our company, nearly all of our prospective customers ran a proof of concept like this, so much so that we once had several team members with the title "Proof of Concept Manager." Today, lawyers increasingly are willing to accept that if many of their peer firms are using Kira, it probably works roughly as expected (over 60% of the Global 100 law firms subscribe to Kira).

Numbers aren't enough to make some people comfortable, though. For them, we are happy to report that you may not need to trust AI to benefit from it. For example, contract reviewers using Kira can still read through agreements page-by-page using the system's built-in document viewer, the same way as they would if doing this work the traditional way. In Kira, however, the reviewers have the advantage of being supplemented by AI. In Figure 1.2, Kira shows the original document, with highlights of information users asked it to find overlaid.

Finally, knowing AI helps build trust. Understanding the possibilities and limitations allows users to learn that AI is not magic, it's software, and software sometimes makes mistakes. Software can do a job or perform a task very

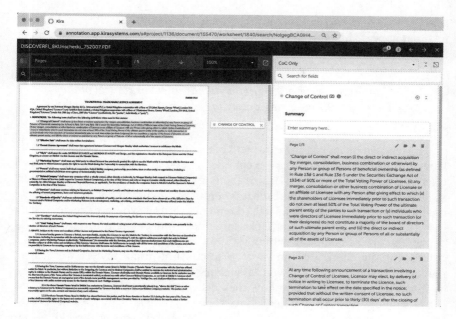

FIGURE 1.2   Kira document viewer.

efficiently as long as you trust in yourself to provide the necessary information, train it to perform specific tasks, and review the results. Trust is earned. Many skeptics rely little on AI when they first start using it, but come to trust it more as they learn how and when it delivers (and when they should count on it less).

Today, AI enhances lawyers, rather than replacing them. AI is helping lawyers do work that they never would have been able to do before. Instead of framing the decision as whether to trust AI or a human lawyer, consider whether you should trust a lawyer doing work the same old way over a technology-enhanced one. We wouldn't.

"What If Our Associates Use the Technology to 'Cheat'?"

Some lawyers worry that—instead of using AI as a supplement—their junior associates will rely heavily on AI to do the work. In other words, they will "cheat" at doing the work. The truth is, there are already non-AI ways to "cheat" at many junior lawyer tasks, and (some) associates use them.

Over our years in and around due diligence contract review, we have heard lots of suggestions on non-AI-ways to do the work faster. You could do a keyword search (ctrl-f) for relevant words such as "assignment" or a phrase like "most favored customer." The problem is that important concepts like "change of control" or "exclusivity" are frequently phrased in nonstandard ways, which makes keyword searching risky. Worse, many contracts for review come in the form of poor quality scans. Keyword searches are hard on text that appears like this, post-OCR:

Mengesnorter iigernent or Control

If-any-material change occurs in the management or control of the Supplieror_the_Business,save accordance-with-the provisions of this Agreement.

Instead, some look at the contract's table of contents for relevant sections. However, based on our years of experience in and around the details of contracts, we can assure you that details sometimes turn up in unexpected places. Section titles work as guides, except when they don't. You could also review a company's filings and financial statements to find where to review. This may work as a supplement but, if used without independent review, you are dependent on the company getting it right the first time.

Essentially, there are non-AI ways to cheat at junior lawyer work. But, they have real limitations. If your associates are going to cheat, they're going to cheat. It's about them, and how they believe law should be practiced, not the technology. Pre-AI, you needed to teach them about why they needed to review documents page-by-page, and not just rely on ctrl-f or the like. Same now, with the popularization of AI. You need to train (and convince) your team to do reviews the right way, whatever that means to you.

"How Are New Lawyers Going to Grow into Great Lawyers with Technology Doing Their Work?"

Talk to an "old timer" (by which we mean anyone from a 30-year partner to a third-year associate) and you're likely to hear about how things were different back when they were getting started, and how that molded them into the amazing lawyer they are today.

Many lawyers care deeply about how the next generation will learn the trade. It's no surprise that they worry that AI will harm lawyer training. With contract review software, for example, we have often heard:

I learned so much about how contracts work and where problems lurked from reading them through, over and over again. How will junior lawyers pick up this same critical skill set?

There are three parts to the answer to this question:

1. *Change is constant.* Lorie Waisberg (Noah's father) joined a 10-lawyer firm in 1970. He learned to be a business lawyer at the elbow of a partner who had been at it for some time. Things were busy, and Lorie was given a lot of responsibility early on. They did every type of corporate law back then,

from incorporating businesses, to securities filings, to M&A. Eventually, they did corporate governance, insolvency, and antitrust. By the time the generation after Lorie joined the firm, it had grown to over 125 lawyers. They were more specialized in subareas; M&A and securities had become different disciplines. While associates still got independent work, stakes were now higher and their scope of independent operations was more constrained. They still developed into excellent lawyers. Noah now has stellar lawyer teammates who learned from someone who learned from Lorie way back when. The way lawyers learn is constantly changing. But they still often turn out all right.

2. *Consider the old way of doing due diligence contract review.* A junior lawyer reads through agreements, page by page, looking for consistent data points (e.g., change of control, assignment, restrictive covenants). Or the old way of doing discovery: junior (or temporary) lawyers scan document after document, saying which are relevant, or which are privileged. Today, thanks to AI, things are different. In contract review, AI directs lawyers to passages that might be relevant, as opposed to spending significant time finding the passages in the first place. Rather than spending lots of time trying to find on-point wording (and sometimes missing it), AI makes users consider whether "Customer will buy 100% of its requirements of paper from Dunder Mifflin" is an exclusivity obligation.

3. *AI is here to stay in law practices.* Many lawyers are using AI now. In 10, 15, or 20 years, when today's junior lawyers become senior lawyers, AI will be a standard part of practicing law. Early experience with AI on the ground level, working elbow-to-elbow (so to speak) with AI tools will equip today's juniors to more fully understand the nuances of AI; they will know what it can and cannot do, when it is more likely to make mistakes, and how to most effectively train it. Even though AI will change and improve over time, "AI-enabled-native" lawyers should have a leg up, as they will be able to understand the technology at a deeper level. Firms that dither about getting on AI now are putting their juniors at a disadvantage for the future.

Legal AI by the Numbers

AI-enabled practice is the way of the future. Juniors need to learn to work this new way. Today, AI is becoming the "market" way much legal work is done. A large number of firms and enterprises use technology assisted review (TAR) in their eDiscovery work. Some 80% of the Global 50 firms use contract analysis software (though within-firm adoption varies). Thousands of firms use AI-powered legal research software. These numbers have grown dramatically in recent years, and will continue to grow.

"Will Using AI Impact (i) My Duty to Keep Client Information Confidential, or (ii) Lawyer–Client Privilege?"

Lawyers have a duty to keep information provided by their clients confidential. Lawyer–client communications are also protected by attorney–client privilege (also known as legal professional privilege, among other names). According to *Black's Law Dictionary,* attorney–client privilege is a "client's right to refuse to disclose and to prevent any other person from disclosing confidential communications between the client and the attorney." Lawyers take this very seriously, and sometimes worry that using AI could cause problems here.

In this respect, AI is no different than many other technologies, like email. Do lawyers worry that they breach client confidentiality or risk the protection of attorney–client privilege by sending confidential information in unencrypted email? No.[1] Does the answer change whether the email is sent via a system hosted on the lawyer's premises or by using a cloud-based application like Gmail or Hotmail? No. AI is just a computer program, so it should be treated identically to email, Word, or Excel. Users put data into Excel, and, using formulas, can even have Excel transform the data. AI software is basically the same: you put data in, and it spits out judgments.[2,3]

Does using cloud technology violate attorney confidentiality obligations or impact privilege? Most, but not all, legal AI software is cloud-hosted. For example, over 85% of Kira subscribers use it in the cloud, though it is also available for on-premises deployment. In nearly every jurisdiction, lawyers are ethically allowed to use cloud software, as long as they take reasonable steps to ensure confidentiality. For example, New York State Bar Association's Committee on Professional Ethics Opinion 842 (from 2010) concludes that "a lawyer may use an online 'cloud' computer data backup system to store client files provided that the lawyer takes reasonable care to ensure that the system is secure and that client confidentiality will be maintained." It went on to list steps that may be included in "reasonable care."[4]

We find that most law firms take security (including doing diligence on vendors) very seriously. To assuage their (understandable) worries, technology vendors take steps, including becoming certified under data security frameworks like SOC2 or ISO 27001.[5] What of attorney–client privilege? Again, using New York as an example, under Section 4548 of New York's Civil Practice Law & Rules, "No communication privileged under this article shall lose its privileged character for the sole reason that it is communicated by electronic means or because persons necessary for the delivery or facilitation of such electronic communication may have access to the content of the communication."[6] In short, lawyer use of AI should not raise any special confidentiality or privilege issues. Since that 2010 ruling, cloud computing has become widely accepted. As of the 2018 ABA Legal Technology Survey Report, the majority of lawyers (55%) have now used cloud computing software tools for law-related tasks.[7]

"Do I Have to Invest a Lot of Time in Training AI to Get Value out of It?"

A common misconception about AI is that it takes a lot of effort training a system to get the most out of it, and that you may not be able to train a system without developers or data scientists involved. While this is sometimes true, it depends on which AI system you are using, and what you need the system to do. While some legal AI requires training, plenty do not. Where training is required, it may be done by using a simple user interface. In other cases, training might need to be done with the assistance of technical experts.

Many problems that lawyers need to solve with the help of AI are fairly common problems having answers that can be defined, such as trying to figure out if someone is an employee or an independent contractor; how a specific judge is likely to rule on a motion; which of a set of documents might be privileged; what a pile of contracts says about data points such as change of control, exclusivity, or confidentiality; or how to know what to do when customer data is breached. If you're in need of help on such common issues, you're not alone. Lots of lawyers—from Biglaw to small firms—need the same answers, and there are well-defined pathways to getting those answers. This has led to a lot of legal AI that comes pretrained to work for common use cases such as litigation analytics, legal research, giving HR law guidance, and contract analysis. The use of out-of-the box trained systems is less common around eDiscovery—where the determinations of what is relevant can be more case-facts specific—though there are pretrained privilege determining systems available.

How comprehensive and robust are these off-the-rack capabilities? Do real lawyers use them? We're most familiar with our own situation at Kira, so we will talk from our experiences. As of September 2020, Kira comes able to identify 1,123 provisions out of the box (e.g., assignment, auto-renewal, additional rent, incurrence of indebtedness covenant), across 40 different thematic groups (e.g., M&A, real estate, employment, banking, accounting, or noncontract use cases like UCC financing statements). Kira also comes pretrained to identify numerous document types and languages. As Figure 1.3 shows, Kira's built-in capability has expanded rapidly in recent years. We expect this to continue. Many of our law firm customers heavily use Kira out of the box. On average, over 75% of their usage is with built-in smart fields.

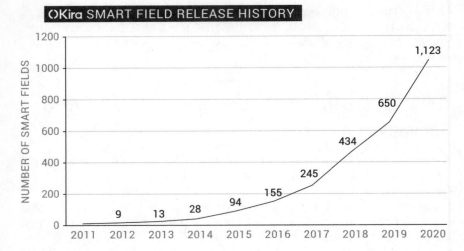

FIGURE 1.3 Kira built-in intelligence: smart-field growth.

Our own built-in smart fields are only part of the story: Kira's users have trained the system to find more than 15,000 additional data points. In the future, we expect many lawyers to choose to share these with others, further expanding Kira's pretrained functionality. So, who trains Kira? We find three main groups:

1. *Firms in some foreign locations have extensively trained Kira for their local language.* This makes sense: today, almost all of Kira's built-in knowledge is for English documents. Kira users in countries like Germany, the Netherlands, Norway, and Brazil have trained Kira to work on their home contracts. Kira has users in over 40 countries, including 10 non-English-first jurisdictions, so there are a number of firms who need to train the system to get maximum use out of it. Though Kira generally does not yet come pretrained in languages beyond English, there are local contract analysis software vendors offering AI software with pretrained clause models in languages including German, French, and Japanese.

2. *Once people get familiar with Kira, they are inspired to teach it more business, or industry-specific concepts.* Industry-specific needs can be regulatory in nature (e.g., for financial institutions that need to comply with global, national, and regional rules) or simply needs that are specific to a vertical (e.g., inventory distribution terms within apparel retailing). There are also endless business-specific needs (e.g., in manufacturing / supply chain management, to find all instances of a particular manufacturer part number or description). Companies are only beginning to

explore all the ways that custom training can benefit their businesses. We believe there is a booming "long tail" of use cases as AI tools like Kira are deployed deeper within companies.

3. *Many people train Kira to represent and capture a specific point of view.* There is tremendous value in training a model specifically on "acceptable" or "standard" language in an agreement. This can allow you to weed out language that doesn't need to be reviewed and save a ton of time. Most law departments now have "playbooks" to encapsulate their points of view on their negotiating position for every major point. Automating these playbooks to correctly route issues for review can save time.

   The other—more profound—reason why you might train Kira to capture a specific point of view is because, frankly, experts do not always agree with each other. You do not need to have attended law school to be familiar with this phenomenon. While most people can agree on the difference between a dog and cat, it takes an expert to give an opinion on whether a photo is of an Alaskan Malamute or a Siberian Husky—and with an imperfect picture, even experts will disagree. In the realm of law, where there is regularly such ambiguity, we see this all the time: one lawyer drafts a termination clause to prevent a customer from canceling their contract early, but then another lawyer sees it as full of holes with easy opportunities for early termination. How should that clause be classified? Does it permit early termination or not? Experts can and do train models to capture their unique insights and expertise. This is something we'll explore further in Chapter 5.

Not every legal AI is the same as Kira. Some will offer more out-of-the-box functionality, some less. For example, legal research and judicial prediction AIs often do not offer users an ability to train them; they just work. On the other hand, many AIs offer or require training.

Why Customize?

Customizing AI can offer advantages. First, it may help you do a task where the AI does not or (like in eDiscovery) could not come pretrained. Second, it can help lawyers amplify their expertise and differentiate against competitors. This is the focus of Chapter 5, so we won't discuss it further here.

When it comes to training AI, there are three possibilities (as shown in Figure 1.4):

1. *It comes pretrained for everything you need.* Examples: litigation analytics, legal research. Many contract analysis, expert systems, and legal prediction systems will come heavily pretrained, but may also offer training interfaces.

PRE-TRAINED	TRAINABLE VIA USER INTERFACE	TRAINING REQUIRED WORKING WITH TECHNOLOGISTS OR PROFESSIONALS
EXAMPLES: LITIGATION ANALYTICS LEGAL RESEARCH	EXAMPLES: KIRA EXPERT SYSTEMS eDISCOVERY TAR SYSTEMS	EXAMPLES: MANY CUSTOM AI PROJECTS

FIGURE 1.4   AI training capabilities.

2. *It is trainable via a user interface.* No data scientists or other technologists are required to intermediate with the trainer's work. Examples: Kira, expert systems, eDiscovery TAR systems.

3. *Training requires working with technologists or professional services.* Often, AI systems require the training be done through working with technologists. Systems built this way sometimes give impressive results on specific narrow tasks (because they have been tailored to work on these), but performance can be brittle (not able to work well beyond the exact intended use case), and further extensions will require working with technologists again. This is not a particularly scalable approach. Examples: many custom AI projects.

The Business Case for AI

Over the past pages, we have covered a number of reasonable, recurring objections to using AI in law practice. Three related objections remain:

- "If AI makes lawyers way more efficient, will we need fewer lawyers?"
- "How does being more efficient work out for me if I bill hourly?"
- "How do I justify the extra expense of the software?"

Our experience has been that these are critical. Where partners are convinced that adopting AI makes good business sense, we often see other objections melt away. Think of a manufacturer like GM or Toyota questioning whether to adopt new technology that enables them to produce an important car component like an engine in half the time. They would be likely to work hard to find a way to implement it. So, in the next chapter, we'll delve into why adopting AI can be financially good, even for hourly billing lawyers.

If you're wondering about Simon, whom we introduced at the beginning of the chapter, his firm is slowly moving into a new way of practicing. Unfortunately, they are already behind their closest competitors in figuring out how to practice law more efficiently, and even in knowing how much it costs them to deliver individual pieces of legal work. To avoid facing similar or even longer odds in the future, they need to accelerate their evolution. Their more sophisticated competitors are certainly not slowing down, and Simon knows that there is no room for complacency. From talking to his peers, and by keeping his eye on the AmLaw 100 rankings, he knows that a firm's position is by no means secure. Firms in the top 10 tend to be stable, but a large share of the firms in the rest of the top 50 have moved up or down significantly over the past dozen years, in both revenue and profitability, and all of them are looking for competitive advantage.

The good news is that Simon's firm has recognized the need to change. We know firms where partners view doing the same work in less time as a silly exercise that leads them to earn less. One example we heard that has stuck with us involved a Biglaw partner asking a knowledge manager at his firm about the status of an automation project by asking how the "PRS" was doing. When the baffled staffer asked what he meant, the partner replied, "the profit reduction system."

The firms and legal teams that are pulling ahead are ones who understand that AI is creating new business models, new economies of scale, and new revenue opportunities that were never thought possible. This is our focus in Chapter 2. Let's dive in!

Notes

1. Should they worry about confidentiality breaches using unencrypted emails? Yes.
2. In this book, we will ignore tech-enabled services, which market themselves as AI but are really work done by people with the assistance of technology. They need to be considered separately, but since this is a book on AI, we will not do so here.
3. We are not aware of anyone seriously questioning whether using Excel or the like impacts confidentiality or privilege, and do not see any distinction with AI (apart, perhaps, from whether training a system raises issues, which we discuss in more detail in Chapter 5).
4. https://nysba.org/ethics-opinion-842/
5. There is a big difference between a vendor being, e.g., "SOC2 certified" and "hosting their application in a SOC2 certified data center." Large hosting providers like Amazon Web Services are usually certified themselves, so—while the latter is better than nothing—it is different than being certified yourselves.
6. NY CPLR § 4548 (2012) NY Civil Practice Law and Rules.
7. Dennis Kennedy's official ABA writeup states, "Actual usage might be higher than the reported usage. For example, many mobile apps are also essentially front-ends for cloud services. Many lawyers who do not think that they are using the cloud may, in fact, be using it every day, especially through mobile apps." https://www.americanbar.org/groups/law_practice/publications/techreport/abatechreport2019/cloudcomputing2019/

CHAPTER 2

#DoMoreLaw: How Doing Work More Efficiently Can Create More Legal Work, Not Less

Alyssa, a young lawyer, showed up at work a few minutes late on a rather ordinary Tuesday, after sitting in traffic en route to the Los Angeles law firm she has been working at for nearly two years. Emerging from the elevator on the 12th floor, the receptionist, Frannie, gave her a peculiar look, as did one of the firm's partners. It was as if they did not expect to see her at all. She was knee-deep in contract reviews, so she quickly headed for conference room 12-E, where she and five of her comrades had been poring over documents for a merger between two film studios. As Alyssa made her way down the corridor, she passed Monica, a paralegal who looked to be on the verge of crying. Alyssa opened the door to the conference room. There they were working diligently, just two of them, robot associates, one wearing Alyssa's identical outfit. It had finally happened. She was, as expected, replaced by a robot. Alyssa screamed in horror. And then she woke up.

Yes, AI can be scary, very scary, but it's not coming for you like *Ex Machina*. In fact, it's opening the door for legal professionals like Alyssa to do more, more interesting work.

Like other industries, there's an ongoing debate on the human impact of AI. However, more and more organizations have come to realize that AI augments lawyers rather than replacing them. It is changing how lawyers work.

By reducing the time-consuming and laborious aspects of their jobs, lawyers are now able to focus on more strategic high-value work.

While that sounds great, there is still a lot of skepticism. After all, if AI makes lawyers so efficient, saving time and money, how can there be more law to be done? We finished Chapter 1 with three unanswered questions:

- "If AI makes lawyers way more efficient, will we need fewer lawyers?"
- "How does being more efficient work out for me if I bill hourly?"
- "How do I justify the extra expense of the software?"

These questions are deeply interconnected, so, instead of treating them individually, we have made them the overall focus of this chapter.

Jevons Paradox: The More Efficient Legal Work Is, the More Legal Work to Do

People often think about how technology will dramatically shrink the amount of work they have to do. They focus on the negatives and zero in on the trimming. They worry about a 60% time savings in one place, 15% in another area, 5% somewhere else, and they see a bleak picture for their own careers. They don't recognize how greater efficiency can drive more work, for both current clients and potential new ones. The demand side for legal work is almost always steadily expanding, due to both (i) an economy that almost always grows over time, plus (ii) a world that is growing ever more complex and regulated. These two factors combine to drive a regularly growing need for legal guidance, whether that means additional research, reviewing details in contracts, having more leases or patents to review, or—even—more lawsuits.

A fallacy in much of the thinking about the growth or decline of legal work lies in equating "legal work" with "work that law firms do." It is true that law firm revenues have been relatively flat or only slightly growing since the Great Recession. Thomson Reuters' Peer Monitor service tracks demand for law firms over time. As you can see in Figure 2.1, after a deep contraction in 2009, growth has floated along just a percentage or two above or below 0% ever since.

But there is more legal work than what law firms do. Technology has enabled more in-house legal departments to retain work in-house, avoiding the premiums that law firms have charged for routine or process-oriented work. An entire Alternative Legal Services (or NewLaw or Law Company) sector has been built up to handle some forms of outsourced legal work, much of which is process-driven and lends itself to technology-enabled services.

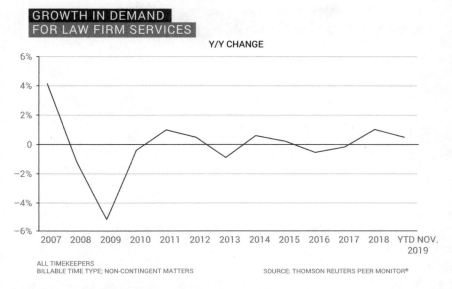

FIGURE 2.1 Growth in demand for law firm services.

Source: From Thomson Reuters, 2019 Report on the State of the Legal Market: Growing Competition Challenging Long-Held Law Firm Assumptions, Legal Executive Institute January 8, © 2019, Thomson Reuters.

The growth in the share of legal work that is retained by in-house legal is hard to measure in dollars, but one proxy for that growth lies in the number of lawyers employed by in-house compared to the number of them employed by law firms. In the United States, the difference is striking. In Figure 2.2, from a July 2018 analysis of the legal industry, it's clear that the growth in in-house employment is exceeding law firm employment by a large margin over 20 years. All the corporations that they work for are doing more and more legal work; it's just that law firms aren't being hired for all of it.

Throw in the legal work that's being performed by Alternative Legal Services Providers (ALSPs) and we see a widening gap between the total demand for legal services and the share of that work that's going to law firms. Much of that work is being retained by in-house departments or sent to ALSPs precisely because those organizations have been willing to apply technology to accomplish more with fewer resources. Law firms willing to make similar investments in technology might be able to claw back some of that gap.

So while this expanding legal market is one reason why we see more work in the future, the more exciting and bigger reason is that efficiency (and the lower unit prices that it brings) opens the door for greater overall demand for legal services.

Technology increases efficiency, resulting in less energy used for a specific task, which creates cost savings. However, demand can go *way* up as unit prices decrease. For example, Henry Ford was able to build a less expensive,

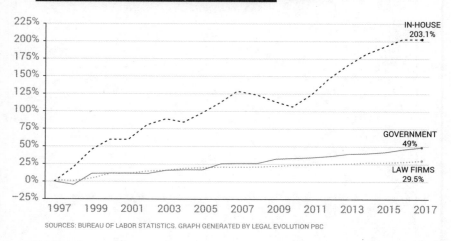

FIGURE 2.2 Percentage change in employed lawyers by practice setting, 1997 to 2017. Source: From Bill Henderson, Our journey to Big (067), September 16, © 2018, Legal Evolution PBC.

mass-produced automobile on an assembly line, which meant fewer jobs assembling each individual car. As aspects of production were performed on a moving assembly, the manufacturing time to produce one Model-T was reduced from 12 hours to 93 minutes, while using less manpower. This pushed the price of a Model T dramatically lower than other cars. In 1911, a Model T cost $700, where average competitor cars cost $1,100. As the Model T's price continued to drop, this drove huge demand. As Wikipedia tells:

> In 1914, Ford produced more cars than all other automakers combined. The Model T was a great commercial success, and by the time Ford made its 10 millionth car, half of all cars in the world were Fords. It was so successful Ford did not purchase any advertising between 1917 and 1923.

More efficient production meant far more automobile production jobs (first at Ford, then elsewhere) were created.

The refrigerator is another great example of how efficiency paradoxically drives more effort (see Figure 2.3). Back in the 1970s, it took some 800 kilowatt hours a year to run a single standard size refrigerator. Today it takes roughly 200 kilowatt hours per year to run a typical refrigerator. And, by the way, today's typical refrigerator is 20% bigger.

Based on refrigerators taking a quarter of the electricity to run, the world must use less energy on refrigeration today, right? Well, no.

FIGURE 2.3   Refrigerator efficiency paradoxically drives more effort.

Source: From Meneghini La Cambusa Refrigerator, available at Robeys 窗

First, increased global standards of living mean people have refrigerators who wouldn't have had them before. For example, in 1995, only about 66% of households in China had a refrigerator. In 2018, 99% did.

The more interesting part of the refrigeration story is how inexpensive refrigeration made it possible for stores to expand their refrigerated foods sections and, as a result, offer a multitude of new products.

The milk section of a well-stocked grocery store once featured skim, half, whole, and chocolate milk. Today, even a random rural supermarket may now feature multiple brands of these classics (including organic and lactose-free versions), plus soy, almond, coconut, rice, oat, hemp, and cashew milk options. Like bake-at-home frozen croissants or baguettes? Okay. What about kale juice? You now have multiple choices! Literally, a convenience store today may have as much refrigeration as a supermarket did back in the 1970s. While it's easy to mock oat milk or kale juice, we are all richer for the choice. Noah remembers the lactose-intolerant kid in his early-1990s summer camp cabin who had to eat his Cheerios with juice, while everyone else got milk. Now, his ailment would be no issue. And—even without *needing* these new products—people happily buy them. Lots and lots of them. Almond milk is expected to reach a USD $6.77 billion market size in 2020. Meaning it must have value for some. Along the way, these new products are creating lots of new food production jobs that never would have existed before.

Affordability led people to buy more refrigerators. Today, it's not uncommon to have a two-fridge kitchen, an extra one in the basement or garage, a separate wine fridge in the kitchen, maybe a bar fridge, too. Plus an additional chest freezer, and perhaps one under the desk in your office. The demand for larger and, in some cases, multiple refrigerators is partially because they are so cheap to buy and run, and partially because there are so many more items to refrigerate today. Just as efficiency increased refrigeration and brought with it a demand for new products, technology-driven efficiency in legal should create demand for more lawyers.

These scenarios illustrate a phenomenon known as the Jevons paradox. Economist William Stanley Jevons saw how, during the First Industrial Revolution, technology was making coal usage more efficient over time. Surprisingly, this led to more coal usage. Efficient technology made coal effectively cheaper to run, leading to more possible uses, counterintuitively increasing overall coal consumption.

An article by author and researcher Darrin Qualman explores the paradox. Qualman discusses lighting and the cost of an hour of illumination. Adjusted for inflation, lighting in the United Kingdom was more than 100 times more affordable in 2000 than it was in 1900. This is because electric power plants are far more efficient, which has driven the price of lighting down. Therefore, the cost of running a single artificial light would be cheaper in 2000 than in 1900. Yet the Jevons paradox once again enters the equation when you look at the significant increase in the need for artificial lighting. As Qualman writes, "The average UK resident in the year 2000 consumed 75 times more artificial light than did his or her ancestor in 1900." Noah remembers his grandmother almost obsessively turning off lights in rooms not in use. Now we light heavily (for better or worse), because the unit cost is so low that it is no longer a barrier.

Law seems ripe for a Jevons paradox increase in usage. Legal services are generally very costly, and consumers have *lots* of unmet legal needs. Costs going down (combined with other delivery changes) could dramatically increase the volume of legal work done.

"Would You Like to Supersize Your Diligence?"

From 1992 to 2004, McDonald's ran a promotion that has remained seared in the public consciousness. For a relatively small amount more money, patrons could "supersize" their meal—getting an even larger fries and soda. After all, why stop at fries that contain 50% your daily recommended fat intake when you can have even more?! While supersizing has not stood the test of time at McDonald's (the 2004 Oscar-nominated documentary *Supersize Me* probably hastened its demise; supersize meals were cut six weeks after the film's premiere), it provides an important lesson in how lawyers who work more efficiently can do more law.

Today, reducing spend on outside counsel is a priority for in-house legal departments. Altman Weil's 2019 survey of chief legal officers is a good source of insight on this. This annual survey asks which "levers" CLOs are pulling to cut spending, and they also ask which of those tactics are most effective. The top two most successful strategies were "outsourcing to non–law firm vendors" (95% saying it drives "significant improvement to cost control") and "shifting law firm work to in-house lawyer staff" (93%). Others include "negotiating price reductions on portfolios of law firm work" (91%); "receiving discounts on law firm hourly rates" (86%); and "using alternative fee arrangements" (82%). Ben O'Halloran, former CLO of a large European private equity–backed company (and previously a senior lawyer at General Electric), says:

> *Law firm services are typically purchased flexibly, on-demand, resulting in a) a market-determined (and entirely valid) pricing premium, and b) limits on knowledge economies that can be achieved (because the on-demand law firm resources continuously vary and are less integrated into the client organisation, its operations and business priorities). Forward-looking legal teams are increasingly approaching legal work flows like process engineers, working to define categories of repeated legal work flows where quality improvements deliver meaningful impacts to the business, and then, where volume is sufficient, to in-source or sole source key parts of those work flows in order to improve quality and efficiency (often with cost savings as well).*

Shifting law firm work to in-house legal staff is an ongoing trend, one that goes against a more general trend toward outsourcing non-core work and services in the corporate sector. The Altman Weil data shows this as well: 36.3% of CLOs anticipated increasing in-house lawyer staff in the next 12 months vs. only 8.5% who were planning staff reductions. In a historical perspective, this study shows that on average, roughly four times as many corporations plan to increase legal staff each year vs. reducing staff since 2010. Thomas Barothy says, "I took over as COO of UBS's legal team in 2017. Since then, we achieved material annual reductions in our spend. Primarily, this has come through expanding our in-house legal team, doing work internally that we used to do externally, and implementing a dedicated outside counsel management team." In a very real sense, a law firm's biggest competitor is often its own clients, as those clients find ways to get better value by solving legal problems themselves with the help of their own staff and technology.

While some clients are after paying less, many seek something that sounds similar, but really is very different: better value legal work. Casey Flaherty (former in-house counsel; consultant to law departments, law firms, and other legal service providers; and author) has extensive experience with legal buy programs, which he says:

> now almost always include large sections in their RFPs on the how, not just the who, of legal service delivery. Lawyer quality remains the threshold consideration. But, once that threshold is passed—once law departments are in the room deciding between the select firms they already deem excellent—lawyer quality stops being decisive. Demonstrable differentiators, including AI usage, can have a significant impact at the margins—and the margins are what matter at the final selection stage.

Rosemary Martin, group general counsel and company secretary of Vodafone adds:

> As a buyer of legal services, I look for value: not necessarily the cheapest option but the one that I think will deliver the outcome I am looking for, be that success in a case, speed in contract execution, or precision in defining the terms of a complex legal relationship.

Ben O'Halloran concurs:

> Legal departments are generally looking to maximise value from all of their spending, whether that be through choices between internal or external resources, process improvements, or deploying new technology. While law firm partners may sometimes interpret the client's objective as mere cost reduction, typically General Counsels are more focussed on improving the value they get from their law firm spending—and that involves both streamlining cost as well as expanding and maximising the potential benefits from outside counsel services.

We know corporate law best, so will go there for an example of how lawyers can provide more value.

Let's consider a $400 million acquisition of a company. Typically, counsel reviews anywhere from 75 to 500 target company contracts during the due diligence process. However, a $400 million company might actually have 5,000–10,000 contracts. Why is such a low percentage reviewed? Is it because there isn't likely to be anything interesting in the unreviewed contracts? M&A lawyers *hope* so. The status quo approach is to review all "material" contracts. Is this an optimal approach? Let's explore further.

Material contracts generally come in two buckets:

1. *High-dollar value or otherwise strategically important contracts.* These tend to be easy to find. You ask the target or their investment bankers which contracts matter, and they give you the list. Then you review them.

2. *Contracts that say something that could be bad for the client.* Sometimes, contracts that aren't otherwise very important say something important. They have a badly drafted buried exclusivity or most favored customer provision in them, which brings in affiliates. Or an out-of-hand indemnity. Theoretically, deal lawyers would like to think that they catch these. But how? You're pretty unlikely to find a problematic provision in contracts you don't review.

In status quo review, only contracts in the first group are reliably reviewed. *Maybe* lawyers review a "sample" of other contracts as part of their review, but this tends not to be a scientifically drawn sample, at least not in a way that Alex and his PhD peers would recognize as a valid approach. Clients may be missing lots of dangerous information, but they and their lawyers would never know.

The only way to be sure is to review the contracts. Why doesn't this happen now? Generally, it's because doing more than a small review is simply not time- or cost-effective for most businesses. Happily, thanks to AI, total diligence is now possible. Rather than a 10% sample, you can now review 25%, 50%, or even 100% of contracts in question, in a manageable amount of time, for an acceptable (though not necessarily low) amount of money. Truth is, a nonrandom sample is often a poor research approach. Yet, many companies are willing to take a chance with it because they believe the odds are in their favor that they won't miss something problematic. In a lot of cases, it works out fine. If, for example, you trigger a change of control clause in a minor software license agreement, it's probably okay. If you breach, you may have to pay a small penalty. Oh well. We've seen this happen, where the client may happily incur a $20,000 penalty instead of spending an additional $300,000 on legal fees to find and avoid penalties like this. They consider it a pretty good risk/reward tradeoff. They're probably right when it comes to avoiding small penalties built into minor contracts. The problem is that contracts can have much worse things in them than this.

More fulsome contract review has different values for financial and strategic buyers. Typically, there are two types of company buyers: financial and strategic. Financial buyers (like private equity firms) are concerned with buying and reselling businesses at a gain. Since they tend to buy businesses and run them as is (in an isolated legal entity), financial buyers are less likely to have issues with a target company's contracts. However, they can still benefit from a faster and deeper review. A faster, light contract review early in the evaluation period can help financial buyers determine which deals to lean into. Also, findings from more thorough diligence can allow financial buyers to more accurately set a fair price for the asset. For example, if an exclusivity clause limits a target's scope of operations, its value may be impaired.

Strategic buyers, on the other hand, add companies they buy into their already-running businesses. This significantly raises the stakes on contract review. Contracts of an acquired entity are equally binding as those the company enters into in the ordinary course of business. Many companies put a lot of effort into ensuring that new contracts they enter into are properly approved. They should be equally careful about contracts they acquire in M&A. Sometimes, really bad things lurk in contracts, even seemingly inconsequential ones. Exclusivity. Non compete. Most favored customer pricing, indemnifications, uncapped liabilities, data transfer restrictions, and other clauses you might never find unless you dig down and look closely. These risks can compound when brought under a large acquirer's significant corporate umbrella. Imagine an emerging beverage company. If things go wrong as it grows, this could wipe out the company, but the company might not be that big so losses are naturally limited. The company is, to a certain extent, "judgment proof." If Coca-Cola or PepsiCo buy them, all of a sudden there is a whole lot more to lose.

The ROI of AI: Explained

Lawyers can add value by using AI to increase the number of contracts they review in transactions. Some clients might be happy to get a lower diligence bill thanks to faster AI-enhanced contract review. But many should be *very* interested in getting twice the diligence for the same price they paid the last time they did a deal, or three times for 30% (or 50%) more money. Figure 2.4 illustrates this. In this simplified example, we assume a 500 contract due diligence contract review, with a reviewer taking an average of 45 minutes a contract reviewing the traditional way, and 20 minutes per contract doing a thorough AI-enhanced review. Kira users consistently tell us they review contracts in 20–90% less time, so this 55% time savings is reasonable. While one review choice could be to use the extra time to reveal all additional contracts as thoroughly as the initial 500 "material" contracts, a better strategy might be to trust the software to spot issues in remaining contracts. While the software might make mistakes here that reviewers won't catch, you miss 100% of the dangerous provisions in contracts you don't review. These additional contracts wouldn't have otherwise gotten reviewed. In keeping with this strategy, we assume all contracts after the initial 500 will be reviewed in 5 minutes per contract. (In fact, a human reviewer would likely spend 1–2 minutes on many of these contracts, and a lot more on a few where the software or their intuition guided them to lean in. Averaging to five minutes per contract overall.) We include report preparation in this minutes-per-contract time assumption, but—likely—client reporting will be pretty slim on the non-material contracts (apart from where something gets found).

FOUR DILIGENCE REVIEW SCENARIOS

	TRADITIONAL	AI ENHANCED DILIGENCE CHEAPER	AI ENHANCED DILIGENCE NEAR SAME COST	AI ENHANCED DILIGENCE SUPERSIZED 35% UP-SELL
CONTRACTS REVIEWED	REVIEW 500 CONTRACTS	REVIEW 500 CONTRACTS	REVIEW 2,108 CONTRACTS TOTAL INCLUDING 500 IN DETAIL	REVIEW 3,248 CONTRACTS TOTAL INCLUDING 500 IN DETAIL
TIME PER CONTRACT	45 MINUTES PER CONTRACT	20 MINUTES PER CONTRACT	20 MINUTES PER CONTRACT FOR 500 CONTRACTS / 5 MINUTES PER CONTRACT FOR ALL ADDITIONAL CONTRACTS	20 MINUTES PER CONTRACT FOR 500 CONTRACTS / 5 MINUTES PER CONTRACT FOR ALL ADDITIONAL CONTRACTS
TOTAL REVIEW TIME	375 HOURS	166.7 HOURS	315 HOURS	410 HOURS
HOURLY FEE	$350	$350	$350	$350
TOTAL FEE (INCLUDING $10/CONTRACT FEE FOR USE OF SOFTWARE)	$131,250	$63,333	$131,336	$175,986

FIGURE 2.4   Four diligence review scenarios.

We assume this is an hourly billing firm, and that the hourly rate for this work is $350 (low for the fanciest US Biglaw firms, but high for small law). We also assume the AI technology costs $10 per contract reviewed. In fact, many contract analysis software offerings are less expensive, but there's no need to shave the numbers too close in this example.

Here, we have four options. Traditional review, where a client gets 500 contracts reviewed for $131,250. AI-enhanced review, where all savings get passed on to the client, and they get the same 500 contracts, this time for $63,333. If the firm agreed with the client to keep roughly to the initial manual review budget but do the work AI-enhanced, they could get 2,108 contracts reviewed, including 500 thoroughly. That's more than 4× coverage. And, if the client was willing to "supersize" their diligence, paying some 35% more than the manual review cost for this work, they could get 3,248 contracts reviewed. Over 6× manual coverage, for 35% more money. Seems like a pretty good value to us, especially if they found anything dangerous in the contracts that would otherwise have been ignored.

Selling risk mitigation is a core skill of many top law firm partners. Upselling more thorough work—whether diligence, or precedent review, or something else—should fall right in their wheelhouse. Supersizing legal work seems unlikely to have a provocative, Oscar-nominated documentary created to criticize it. Instead, it will leave clients happy about paying their lawyers more money. Does upselling actually work? From 2017 to 2020, the average number of documents in a cloud project inside Kira has doubled. Though there are a few reasons this might be so, we think the most likely explanation is that people are doing bigger projects now because AI technology allows them to.

There's another piece to this puzzle; we didn't cover realization rates in the example above. We suspect the lawyer might have an easier time getting paid in full in the AI-enhanced situations. Improved realization rates are a core way hourly billing lawyers can do better financially through doing more efficient work. On average, US Biglaw firms have an 89% realization rate. That means that after discounting off their standard rate and reducing the hours billed to accommodate client demands, firms are leaving on average 11% of their potential billings on the table. Beyond that, many clients will write off additional charges, resulting in an even lower collected realization rate. In fact, this overall number hides important details. Clients often view partners—even very expensive ones—as good value. (As clients ourselves sometimes, we generally think they're right.) On the other hand, some clients refuse to pay for junior lawyers. Some practice areas have better realization rates than others. For example, in American bankruptcies, bills are approved by the US trustee, which is much less aggressive on law firm bills than a Fortune 500 legal ops or procurement team.

Figure 2.5 shows how AI use can impact realization rates. We will imagine a different AI-enhanced project from the one considered in Figure 2.4. Here, in scenario 1, a firm bills its client $200,000 for some junior lawyer work. In fact, the partner wrote off 20% of the amount their associates worked on this project before even sending the $200,000 bill, because they didn't think the juniors worked efficiently, and they worried about upsetting the client and damaging their relationship. These write-offs are common. Despite this preemptive write-off, the client only paid 65% of the diligence fee, still feeling that the work wasn't done efficiently. (The client is right!) Eventually, after lots of haggling, the firm got paid $130,000. Now, consider the AI-enhanced scenario 2. Here, the partner feels good about the efficiency of their team, so they bill all hours worked: $250,000. Throughout the matter, and in delivering the bill, the partner explains how their firm is focused on efficiency, and the client is happier about the value of the work they received. To be conservative, we assumed only a 10-point jump in realization rate, though—if the partner is good at selling value—this might be higher. Here, because the bill was higher (due to no preemptive write-off) and because of the

INCREASING REALIZATION RATES

SCENARIO 1		SCENARIO 2	
TRADITIONAL WORK		AI ENHANCED	
DUE DILIGENCE FEE	$200,000	DUE DILIGENCE FEE	$250,000
WRITE-OFF RATE	20%	WRITE-OFF RATE	0%
REALIZATION RATE (OF JUNIOR LAWYER'S WORK)	65%	REALIZATION RATE (OF JUNIOR LAWYER'S WORK)	75%
		COST OF AI	$10,000
TOTAL PAID BY CLIENT	$130,000	TOTAL PAID BY CLIENT (LESS COST OF AI)	$177,500

FIGURE 2.5   Increasing realization rates.

higher realization (collection) rate, the firm makes an extra $45,500, despite us assuming that the AI cost $10,000. That's 35% more revenue! And—to keep the numbers simple—we didn't even look at matter profitability here. Suffice it to say that throwing out hours—either because you don't bill them or the client doesn't pay for them—is bad for profitability. Changes in realization rates can *really* make an impact. If a firm has an industry average 89% realization rate, and has over $1 billion (or $10 million, for that matter) in revenue, the money (and profit) it is leaving on the table can be pretty *immense*.

While the previous example was centered on hourly billing lawyers, fixed-fee work is getting more and more popular. In some jurisdictions, like the United Kingdom and Brazil, we believe the majority of transactional work (including due diligence contract review) is fixed fee. In a fixed-fee situation, lawyers who can generate the same amount of output with less effort are going to make more profit. Fixed-fee work can even be very profitable for firms, even at lower prices, if the firms get more efficient. Happily, there tends to be *lots* of room for more efficient work in law practice. If we remember the plight of poor Simon G. from Chapter 1 (whose firm lost its longstanding panel position with a key client), fixed fees (coupled with efficiency) are likely part of how Simon's equally prestigious competitors were able to so severely undercut his firm . . . and how Simon and his firm can fight their way back onto the panel next time.

Law firms can also realize ROI from AI by using their efficiency in their pitches. AI users tell us that AI has helped them win new work and retain work that might have otherwise gone to lower-cost providers. Law firms spend huge amounts to win new business. Noah's old firm, for example, threw (wonderful!) lavish parties for alumni. One was at the Central Park Zoo and included a seal feeding partway through. While Noah would like to think that they hosted him and his ex-colleagues just to catch up, he suspects the real purpose was to drive deals and litigation projects from alums who had moved in-house. While law firms don't all rigorously measure wins from using AI, others do. In 2016, Ragu Gurumurthy, Deloitte's chief innovation and chief digital officer, stated in a CNBC video, "[Kira] has tangibly enabled us to generate about $30 million of new revenue that we would not have generated otherwise." The impact of winning new business or retaining work that might have gone elsewhere can be very significant, easily covering all the time you spend reading this book, its cost, and the (much more significant) time and materials costs of implementing AI. Ultimately, delivering good value is good business. It's even better than putting on a fancy party.

Corporates who deploy legal AI tend to realize value in two ways. Many use AI to do work more efficiently. Since—for most businesses, apart from those that bill hourly—there's a strong view that doing the same work in less time is better, this is a pretty easy way to realize a return on investment. The more interesting way corporates find value is by being able to use AI to uncover information they wouldn't have been able to find without it. This can enable companies to make better, more informed business decisions and nimbly respond to environment changes. Here, the benefits can be hard to measure, but enormous.

Value Is in the Eyes of the Beholder

A satisfied client is someone who feels that their money was well spent. Remember the famous tracking shot through the kitchen in *Goodfellas*, as Henry and his date Karen enter the legendary Copacabana Club in New York City to The Crystals singing "Then He Kissed Me"? Doors are flying open ahead of them, as waiters scramble to grab a table and chairs and anchor them front and center in the best location in the house, before breaking out the finest wine. Now that's first-rate service and good value even at a price beyond what money can buy.

Many of us have encountered situations where we have spent more than usual and walked away saying, "It was well worth it." Value need not be expensive—maybe it's buying a box of Afeltra linguine for $6.90 (or even Barilla for $1.99), instead of Signature SELECT brand for $0.69. Value is all about feeling you did well for the money spent, relative to other choices. Danny Meyer (among New York's leading restaurateurs) believes that value can be had at any price; you just have to know how to find and package it. Meyer and his team have found great success at a range of price points, from fine dining at Gramercy Tavern and Union Square Cafe to the popular jazz clubs Blue Smoke and Jazz Standard, to 249 Shake Shack fast-food eateries. Meyer says, "Essentially, what's going to determine how you succeed in New York is how the people feel about the space, how good the food is, how they perceive the value, and most importantly how they feel treated."

Success in law, as in other service industries, is not just about price; it's largely about how clients feel about your experience (or that of the firm), how good the advice is, and how well they've been treated. Legal services are ripe for delivering clients better value work, because so many component parts are done slowly and not very well. This means that lawyers can potentially charge more and yet have clients walk away happier than they were when they were paying less.

MISSION (IM)POSSIBLE

By Dr. Thomas Laubert, Vice President and Group General Counsel, Daimler AG; Dr. Pietro Brambilla, Head of Digital Transformation Integrity and Legal, Daimler AG; and Dr. Jörg Hanke, Skadden, Arps, Slate, Meagher & Flom LLP

Picture this—you have been tasked with supporting the largest business reorganization project in years: the transformation of the company's two main operative business divisions into two legally independent entities by way of a hive-down. This means ensuring that all permits, authorizations, contracts, etc. required to conduct the respective businesses need to be validly transferred to the relevant new entity and/or amended or newly obtained. Any impediments such as change of control provisions, transfer restrictions, and obligations in connection with the consummation of the transaction (e.g., information or consent requirements) need to be identified. The framework conditions are demanding:

Time frame: one year to signing

Team: lean as possible

Documents to review: approximately 1 million active legal documents, such as contracts, certificates, and permits

By conservative procedure: mission impossible

Looking back to spring 2018, Daimler AG had decided to strengthen its customer focus and to increase the group's agility by separating the car and van and the truck and bus businesses into two new subsidiaries—internal project name: "Project Future." Upon consummation of the hive-downs, the new Mercedes-Benz AG would control the global business of Mercedes-Benz Cars & Mercedes-Benz Vans and the new Daimler Truck AG would be responsible for the global truck and bus business. Daimler AG, as the parent company, would be responsible for governance, strategy, and control functions, and would provide groupwide services. To achieve this, each of these entities would be required to be fully operational immediately upon effectiveness of the hive-down. It was an enormous effort in which the legal department also played a decisive role, especially regarding the necessary contract management.

Typically, a traditional approach to a large project like this might involve reviewing somewhere between 20,000 and 200,000 documents, which could take (at the upper end) more than 50 people working for approximately one year at the review and need a very large budget. How would we review one million documents and accomplish it in the expected time frame? Even with a super-heavy lift, a 200,000-contract review would only reveal what was in 20% of the documents. What about the other 80%? Should we decide to just look at samples and hope for the best?

This project demonstrated clearly that traditional ways of resourcing legal work might no longer be sufficient to deliver on business objectives. The traditional way also did not fit with the DNA of Daimler or the philosophy of its legal department. For more than 130 years, Daimler has been moving people and goods all over the world—safely, efficiently, comfortably, and with innovative technologies that have always kept the company a step ahead of the competition. It is this spirit that also drives the work of the legal department.

Innovation and technological change has been an integral part of the strategy of the Daimler legal function for many years. As such, we had the advantage that we already had created a specialized technology team within the legal department. Its aim is to promote the use of innovative technologies to drive automation, reduce complexity, increase speed, and improve efficiency in order to free up legal colleagues for more strategic and transformative work.

"Project Future" was a perfect opportunity to demonstrate the relevance of this transformative approach for the largest projects on hand—and to show that modern technologies such as artificial intelligence (AI) can take the importance of the legal department for the business colleagues to a new level. An important part of the better value equation when leveraging innovative technology is volume, and with AI you have the opportunity to accomplish what was never considered possible so far, such as creating a complete picture of a large document landscape.

Together with Skadden, our law firm commissioned for the project, we scanned the market and selected the contract review and analysis software from Kira Systems to do an AI-enhanced review of all active legal documents. To do this project, the legal team needed to train the software to find the information and legal concepts they sought in German and to verify if the prebuilt modules in English were sufficient for their purposes. Such training requires a certain number of documents providing for positive and negative samples.

IT infrastructure (Daimler preferred not to upload all data to an external cloud but to use an on-premise system) and all users had to be set up so everything was ready to go, all in short order. We did not always have sufficient samples to train the software for every legal concept (e.g., certain types of permits); nevertheless, the software still proved valuable for review purposes.

In the course of the review, it became clear that, worldwide, there were far more legal documents on file than initially expected. In sum, the 1 million that were initially expected to be reviewed was only 25% of the 4 million active documents. However, the project team kept their heads down and got it done.

Despite the massive volume, the review team consisted of less than 10 people. In order to ensure the best quality, the first-level review team checked approximately 80,000 of the most important legal documents manually with the help of the software. By that system, potential issues were highlighted that helped to focus on the relevant provisions and to speed up the review. All other documents were primarily analyzed by the software. The flagged provisions were just reviewed by a so-called first-level team, which also curtained related sections as well as a pre-agreed number of the other documents for quality check purposes. The team was supervised by senior lawyers who made decisions in cases of doubt. In addition, a second-level review team carried out quality checks throughout the whole volume of documents. Over the review period, trust in the capability of the software and the trained modules increased more and more, and consequently, the number of quality checks could be reduced.

In the process, the Daimler and Skadden team found meaningful information in contracts that never would have surfaced if only 20% of the documents had been reviewed (or, more realistically, 5%, given the emergence of a larger document universe than initially expected). Unsurprisingly, low-priority contracts were less likely to contain unexpected information. However, even these types of contracts provided for certain clauses requiring further action in order to consummate the hive-down (e.g., to inform a counterparty or to obtain a counterparty's consent).

In the end, the review team was able to finish the challenging task with a far more thorough picture of all of the contracts held by the company than would have been possible without the help of AI.

Mission accomplished.

This massive undertaking is a great illustration of the sheer volume of work that can be achieved by using AI. In an increasingly complex world facing an exponential growth of information, one needs exponential technology that is able to deal with these new challenges.

What else did we learn from the project?

Data is the foundation for AI. Having good qualitative and quantitative data sets is a prerequisite for running a successful AI project. This is why we have further strengthened our overall data and information strategy with a dedicated Data Officer for our organization. In addition, we are focusing our efforts on the targeted adoption of AI technology to have the greatest transformative impact with limited resources.

The use of AI clearly empowers people in the legal department to do higher-value work. However, innovation and transformation doesn't happen overnight. Driving digital transformation really takes a lot of commitment, because it is not just as simple as buying software and getting people on the team to open the application. It is equally important to foster behavioral change as well.

The close cooperation between internal and external lawyers enhanced by powerful modern technology turned this initial "Mission Impossible" to one of our most successful and efficient projects of the legal department in recent years. It clearly demonstrated the added value that a modern legal department can bring to the entire company.

Access to Justice

There are well over a million lawyers in the United States. More than 150,000 barristers and solicitors in England and Wales. More than 130,000 in Canada. Over 160,000 in Germany. Some 800,000 in Brazil. Yet, in all these places, many people go without a lawyer when they need one. A June 2017 *Washington Post* article noted that approximately 80% of low-income individuals in the United States cannot afford the legal assistance they need, while 40–60% of the legal needs of the middle class go unmet.

The American Bar Association cites access to justice as one of the fundamental principles of the rule of law. In a December 2017 article on ABA.com called "Access to Justice: Mitigating the Justice Gap," Leonard Wills wrote:

> *Access to justice consists of the "ability of individuals to seek and obtain a remedy through formal or informal institutions of justice for grievances." This process usually requires individuals to obtain legal representation—or at a minimum, legal advice. Without legal assistance, individuals can struggle to navigate through the complexity of court procedures. An individual's failure to understand court procedures and the substantive law-related issues of their case can lead to the loss of a home, children, job, income, and liberty.*

Access to justice is a problem, but it is also an opportunity. If lawyers could figure out how to package and price their services in a more appealing way, there is a vast latent market that could use much more legal service than they get today. AI (by driving more efficient work) can be part of the equation that enables lawyers to deliver legal services at a price current nonconsumers will be willing and able to pay.

Some Biglaw lawyers may have tuned out over the last few paragraphs. What does serving the poor and middle class have to do with them (apart from their pro bono program)? Well, even the biggest companies in the world let many potential legal problems go unsolved, finding the price to value equation not compelling. Think! Where do your clients face risk, or could use help, that they're currently ignoring because of cost, complexity, or speed? What if you could do the work for a third, tenth, or twentieth the cost? Or give an answer 10 times faster? Would that make clients pay attention to this area of concern? If so, then start to think about how. AI and other innovations may make executing on this opportunity possible.

ACCESS TO JUSTICE: A PRODUCT-MARKET FIT PROBLEM

By Jack Newton, CEO and Founder, Clio

Law and the legal system are an integral part of how our society operates. Yet we know that not all citizens of our society are able to access it. In fact, data from the World Justice Project shows that 77% of US citizens who encountered a legal issue did not have that issue resolved by a lawyer. Yet over 80% of lawyers tell us the number one thing they need in their law firm is more clients to grow revenue. Any economist would look at this with raised eyebrows—with such massive demand on the consumer side, lawyers should be complaining about having too many clients. Instead, legal is an inefficient market where supply is not effectively meeting demand.

There are many contributing factors to the state of the legal industry, many of which were heavily exposed during the COVID-19 pandemic. You have a court system that is slow moving and inaccessible to many people, at least in part because it has not evolved to stay in step with technological changes (an issue well-known long before the strain of a pandemic). On the consumer side, many people do not reach out to a lawyer because they perceive them to be inaccessible, expensive, and difficult to work with. When you consider that 40% of Americans would struggle to come up with $400 for an unexpected expense, it is not surprising that legal services would be out of reach. And, when you look at the data, legal services are not priced or packaged in a way that is financially feasible to most consumers.

While there is no silver bullet when it comes to solving the access to justice issue, there are many ways we can improve it. The biggest one is adopting technology. A technology-enabled lawyer can help more clients, without sacrificing their livelihood, by increasing accessibility to legal services and automating their administrative work so they can spend more time practicing law.

Using technology for the benefit of clients and legal professionals should be table stakes for any law firm. Yet there are still too many firms that view their address and the size of their boardrooms as the most important part of their client's experience. But when you consider how much more cost-effective it would be to deliver legal guidance through a Zoom chat as opposed to a meeting in a downtown office space with a marble-lined lobby, the numbers just make sense.

Technology can enable law firms and lawyers to deliver their legal services by increasingly working from their home offices, from a co-working space, or from remote locations. That dramatically changes the underlying cost structure of running a law firm. Combined with the productivity enhancements that technology can bring to a law firm through practice management software, document automation software, AI, and contract review software (to name just a few), lawyers can provide greater value to customers who would rather pay for results than ambiance. And lawyers can enjoy a more flexible working life that is not bogged down with pen-and-paper time tracking or wet signatures.

The access-to-justice problem does not exist in a vacuum—it is for all of us to solve. The good news is that it represents a huge opportunity for lawyers willing to adapt to a new way of thinking. The ability to deliver legal services in a new way, coupled with the productivity enhancements that technology can provide, allows lawyers to offer a completely different cost structure to the market and increase the accessibility of their legal services to everyone. This is simply a product-market fit problem, and one that the legal industry has the power to change.

CHAPTER 3

The Small Law Mindset

Bringing Biglaw Capabilities to Smaller Firms

While lawyers in large and small firms are fundamentally solving similar legal problems, the business of Biglaw and small law (typically firms of 20 people or less, down to solo lawyers) have almost nothing in common. Biglaw is often about serving massive corporations. Sometimes you're dealing with RFPs and things like that. It's not that small law firms never represent big corporations. In some sectors, that's how it works. But for the most part, small law just doesn't look very much like Biglaw. Not to say that small law is small. Solo- and small-firm lawyers together make up more than half of the lawyers in the US today.

One primary example of the difference between Biglaw and small law is observable in the systems and practice end of the business. Lawyers in small law firms don't just practice law. As is the case in most small businesses, they need to wear many hats. Working in a small law firm often means you'll have to be part of the marketing team, leadership, operations team, and perhaps even have to moonlight as tech support. Ironically, many legal tech companies promote their business by telling lawyers: "Our product will let you get back to what you do best, practice law." The truth is, unless their product handles everything else from marketing to IT to administrative tasks to meeting new clients, it's not going to take over. It can, however, make life much easier. Nonetheless, it's rare to find people at small firms who can actually just focus

....

This chapter comes heavily from Sam Glover (founder, former CEO, and editor-in-chief of Lawyerist.com) conveying his perspective on AI in small law to Noah and Alex. He has much more knowledge about this important area than they do, and Noah and Alex thought it would be better to defer to him (and Carolyn Elefant, who wrote the "Being a Practical Technologist" sidebar in this chapter).

on practicing law. And it's virtually impossible for a solo practitioner, who by default has other hats to wear. That's okay. For people who are interested in the business of law as well as the accompanying technology, juggling the various hats behind the business is what they enjoy.

Another commonality among small businesses, in general, is that there is usually greater flexibility. Small businesses, including law firms, are often able to think and act outside the box more readily than larger firms, and for this reason, you may see greater innovation, as necessary. Remember, "Necessity is the mother of invention."

One of the reasons that successful lawyer communities like Lawyerist (which Sam Glover co-founded in 2009, and which focuses on small firms and technology) became popular is because there are so many external factors, from the latest technology to new business models, that have an impact on how law is practiced, especially for small firms and solo practitioners.

To AI or Not to AI?

When it comes to AI, there is still some fear, uncertainty, and doubt. Sam Glover recalls his first foray into this technology:

> I remember when I was first introduced to AI. The salesman said, "Let's say you wanted to understand what your choice of law provisions are going to be in a huge document dump with thousands of documents." He then pressed a button and it generated a PDF document with the choice of law provisions indexed and identified across this huge document database. It basically gave me a bunch of data about a larger bunch of data in a matter of minutes. I kind of shrugged my shoulders, because I figured that's what it's supposed to do. And then it hit me: I would have needed a legion of attorneys to gather that same information from the documents; it would have taken hours of work. We tend to take for granted what technology can do and how fast it can do it.

And he's right; think about doing a search on a case 20 years ago. Those of us who remember the pre-internet world know how long it would have taken at the law library to find the various articles and documents associated with the case.

Clearly, AI is now making a difference for the legal community. Litigation-focused firms of all sizes are leveraging technology assisted review (TAR) in their eDiscovery work. Small firms are now using contract analysis software to realize significant time savings. And they're using advanced AI to power their legal research, which is leveling the competitive playing field. The use of chatbots is also a way that AI is making its way into small firms, which can be used as a backup to decision trees or as a replacement for them. Chatbots can also assist in trying to help answer client questions quickly, to free lawyers up for big-picture concerns.

Yet, while the smaller firms and solo attorneys would likely be less risk-averse to trying newer technology, they are not always in a position to do so. Larger firms can afford IT departments that can introduce the latest technology, figure it out, and train attorneys, provided there is a consensus to do so. They also have the data to justify the expense.

Smaller firms and solo attorneys may want to bring in the new technology, but they may or may not have the budget or the time to climb the learning curve. So, if you're in a firm with three lawyers, a paralegal, and perhaps a receptionist, the software usually needs to be something that you can use, and get value from, right out of the box. In essence, technology needs to be boring (aka, dispersed to the masses) for most small law firms to add it to their repertoire. For example, we no longer think about the fact that we're all walking around with these powerful tools in our pockets that can do all kinds of amazing stuff, and yet we are.

In this way, solo and small firms are a lot like the masses, where the technology needs to be useful and cost-effective, so much so that it just becomes part of what they do.

Once you see what AI can do, the fear and concern are no longer about how well the technology works, but whether or not AI will prove to be cost-effective and beneficial over the long term. You don't want to be like the parents who buy their kids a remote control drone or 90-room dollhouse for their youngster that takes six hours to assemble and will occupy the child for about 90 minutes before they either get bored or crash the drone into their neighbors' garage. You want something that will keep working for you even once it gets boring.

It's All about Practicality

Most often, small firms are not shopping for AI to be competitive in the marketplace; they tend to take a more practical approach. Rather than having a specific AI strategy, which may be the case with a larger firm, for the small firm it comes down to the ever-prominent consumer question: "What can this do for me?" If you think of the typical small law consumer, it goes back to the concept mentioned above: "Technology really becomes interesting when it's boring."

Some lawyers also find that AI enters their small firms through other technology. For example, Casetext has its Cara tool, so that if you want to quickly look at cases that you can cite in order to respond to a brief, you can just upload your opponent's brief and it will spit out a profile of the case law that you need to respond to. It's super useful, super easy to use, and powered by a machine learning algorithm on the back end. That's one effective way of using AI. It's also affordable and easy to use, making it a good value. Again, as with small businesses in any field, small law firms and solo attorneys insist on getting good value. They cannot afford not to be vigilant.

BEING A PRACTICAL TECHNOLOGIST

By Carolyn Elefant, Owner and Principal Attorney, Law Offices of Carolyn Elefant PLLC, and Blogger at MyShingle.com

I've been practicing law for over 30 years, since graduating from Cornell Law School in 1988. After a few years of working for the government and large firms, I decided to go out on my own. Working from home, long before it was fashionable, forced me to become an early adopter of technology and to explore new ways to meet lawyers who might refer me business—since in-person networking in downtown DC wasn't convenient from where I lived. So, in 2002, I started a blog, MyShingle.com, to share my ideas on solo and small law firm practice. Though my goal of interacting with other lawyers through the blog was initially dashed (my site attracted about 10 readers on a good day), today my blog draws as many as 25,000 readers a month. When it comes to technology, my sense is that many solo and small firms are still wrapping their heads around AI and, like most of us, trying to differentiate between AI and the rest of technology. As for me, I consider myself a practical technologist. It doesn't matter as much what is powering the technology tools as to whether they work and serve my goals.

Like many of my colleagues, I am a busy practicing lawyer so I don't have time to spend a day learning something new. Nor do I have a tech consultant on staff to help me out. So to make my technology selections, I apply a 10-minute rule. This means that if I can't figure out how to use a tech product in 10 minutes, I will probably not employ it in my practice.

Be Practical

I counsel solo and small firm lawyers to, above all else, be practical in their approach to technology and match their needs to the product. For example, if a lawyer handles a dozen appeals each year, she won't need the same degree of automation as a busy personal injury attorney with a high-volume, template-based practice. There are fewer tools for small firms and solo attorneys than for large firms mostly because they don't require as much data and/or it's not as cost-effective. That said, solo and small-firm lawyers need to stay abreast of technology to avoid becoming outdated. Lawyers who were content to keep paper files found themselves scrambling during the COVID-19 pandemic when forced to go remote overnight. In addition, 37 states impose a technology competence requirement, which means that solo and small lawyers must educate themselves on the benefits and risks of technology to serve clients. These days, resources abound for solo and small firms seeking to learn about tech solutions—from informal chats on Facebook groups, to bar association CLE programs, to legal tech podcasts, to blogs. In most respects, I think that I am typical of many solo and small-firm practitioners: I learn tech on a need-to-know basis, often on the fly in informal groups or at conferences. Although, on a theoretical level, I am intrigued by AI and believe that it's important for lawyers to be cognizant of AI applications when they impact our clients (think AI-powered recidivism sentencing tools that have built-in biases), ultimately, solos and smalls want solutions that will help right away, whether powered by AI or not.

Looking Ahead

In terms of where we go with AI, solo and small firms have different needs than large firms. Whereas many Biglaw attorneys are obsessed with predictive tools for both eDiscovery and legal research, these products have little relevance to many solo and small firm lawyers. That's because many small-firm lawyers practice in lower-level courts handling family law, small criminal matters, and trusts and estates. There, many cases are decided by a judge on the bench without a written opinion. So the data necessary to predict how a local judge might rule on a small matter simply doesn't exist. Solos are further limited with predictive models because an individual firm can't handle the volume of cases needed to produce data that would make prediction accurate.

I'd like to see more AI tools that can actually help solo and small firms get work done faster. There is one company for example that has developed a program that will generate all necessary case discovery documents from a complaint. This would be a huge cost saving for small firms. Sure, using AI to help with "back-end" operations—such as automating email responses or running a targeted marketing campaign—is a huge benefit to solos, but ultimately, I'd like to get to the point where AI applications can be used to improve the quality of the substantive work that solos and smalls do because that above all would increase meaningful access to justice.

What Does Your Future Market Look Like?

AI is not just about what tools to buy, but how you approach incorporating it into your business. "When I talk to somebody who is looking for advice on how to start a law practice right now, one of the first things I tell them is to be skeptical of going out and talking to other lawyers, or clients, about how they've done things in the past. Bottom line is, we're not in the past anymore. We're already in the future and we need new business models and people who are willing to look and ask: How can I do the best job for my clients going forward? What does this market want from me now? And what is the market going to look like in 5 or 10 years? And then build that firm, go into business, or hang out your shingle," says Glover.

There's a really important mind shift change today that anyone who wants to be successful should adopt. It starts with asking yourself: how can I get things done? That is in the future tense. Instead, we are too often focused on how we do things in the present, which is often based on the past.

You should look for technology that helps solve the problems that already exist for you and your clients. If you start by considering problems, you will come up with good solutions that involve technology because that's where the world is. When you come in with a deep understanding and empathy for what clients want out of the attorney–client relationship, what they're hoping to accomplish, what they need from you, and what problems they are experiencing, you will then see AI as a possible solution. Other tools, or solutions, won't be AI-based at all. That's okay, too. Get what you need and don't let the latest hyped tech products dictate what your practice should look like. People at all levels of law, and in other industries, get sucked in by hype and what technology is capable of doing without determining whether or not it's something that solves their specific problems. Get what you need, not what you're told you need.

Technology, such as AI, should also fit smoothly into your business process. In the design world, you talk about requirements. For example, you'll decide that what is being designed must be made out of wood or the door handles or entrances have to be ADA compliant. It's a good idea to have parameters and constraints in mind when you think about developing your practice. For example, you might decide: I'm going to have a home office, I'm working only on a flat fee basis, I'm not going to have employees, I'm only going to work with contractors, I will not take on more than X number of clients at any given time, I'm never going to start something that hasn't been predrafted for me, and so forth. Whatever it might be, spending time thinking about the requirements, parameters, and constraints that you want to establish for yourself and your practice is important. This will also spill over into your life— this, too, is important, as too many lawyers are working themselves into high levels of stress, which can become physically dangerous and unhealthy. You may want to set up parameters, requirements, and constraints for life, such as not working more than 40 hours a week except in extreme circumstances, not taking work home on weekends, or making sure you take two solid weeks of vacation during the year, interrupted only in an emergency. Technology can help with your parameters and constraints. You can build and maintain a much healthier and more successful practice if you come in with a tech-friendly attitude and let tech help create the type of practice that you want.

Plan for the Future Before It Arrives

Technology is built and typically sold in present time. These applications, however, may not be what you will be looking for when the future arrives and you need technology that solves your problems. Be realistic and practical. For example, flying cars have been dreamed about since the 19-teens. Yet they never got off the ground, so to speak. The far less complicated cell phone was not commonly found in old sci-fi books or films. The future is hard to predict, but you can make some educated guesses as to what you may need in the future by looking at what needs you have now and what changes and developments are taking place around you. For example, the global market is growing, and the need to quickly and accurately translate legal documents into various languages is already becoming a "future is now" scenario.

Often we only look at our current needs, and on occasion we think about how much smoother our businesses could run if we changed them. As a result, a lot of the changes that people have to make now could have benefited them five years ago.

For years there has been a push for the paperless office. When the COVID-19 pandemic first hit the United States, there were still many lawyers who couldn't work from home because they still had the papers they needed in their offices. Suddenly they were scrambling to do the things they should have been able to do years earlier, or at least had the mechanism in place to make a smooth transition.

A lot of people learn this way. Something needs to happen before they turn to technology. Many business owners did not have backups of their business files and documents when Hurricane Katrina hit. Those who were prepared in case something happened had an easier time reopening. Others had a difficult road ahead of them. Some businesses never returned at all. Backups might have enabled them to keep going.

In some cases, you can build software around an idea, based on the problems you are having. It might mean bringing in the technical expertise, but it's entirely possible. For example, Counter Tax Lawyers, based in Toronto, Canada, is a small firm made up of tax attorneys, legal experts, mathematicians, and technology experts who deal with a variety of tax issues. They pooled their knowledge and created Counter Tax software, to help attorneys "work more efficiently, conduct deeper analysis, clarify your decisions, and yield better results," as they put it.

For companies like Counter Tax, or others that create their own software, they want to provide a manner of responding to the problems that lawyers face with access to faster, efficient, more affordable data. What's happening today is that innovative attorneys can now create software with technical help, which is essentially how Kira Systems started its document review software. It came from a problem that needed to be solved—too many lawyers spending an inordinate amount of time on contract reviews rather than putting their high level of skills to better use while AI handled such reviews.

You can really set yourself apart by being innovative, but you need to act quickly. Keep in mind that there's a very limited amount of time between what's innovative now and when everybody catches on. You want to get out ahead of the field and really distance yourself from the pack. That's how innovation begins in the legal field or other industries, with visionaries who have ideas and a vision of the future . . . and act on it.

Small firms have even greater incentives to devise their own software solutions because they know that their niche market may be underserved by the major software companies that are selling to the larger law firms. There's something to be said for fighting in your own weight class, and that's often the case with smaller firms who represent smaller businesses and need the tools to fight at their own level.

In the end, it's pretty simple: there is so much potential for small firms to take advantage of AI technology. The problem is that it requires lawyers to get away from just focusing on their biggest pain points and instead focusing on what their pain points will be in the future. If you're not using AI technology, then you're just competing with other lawyers who are playing in the same ballpark that they've been playing in for decades. But if you figure out how to innovate and set yourself apart, you're no longer competing with other people, you are taking the lead. Small and solo attorneys can, and should, stay ahead of the pack by focusing on the possibilities that will work for them, in AI and in technology in general.

CHAPTER 4

AI: A Modern Job Creator

The New Legal Mindsets, Skill Sets, and Jobs That Are in Demand

Introduction by Corinne Geller
Director of Legal Knowledge Engineering, Kira Systems

As a new parent, the demands of working in private practice, including the unpredictability of my schedule, made it quite difficult to put my best foot forward in either role. I had completed a bachelor of commerce as my undergraduate degree and a Masters of Business Administration in addition to my law degree, so I sought to find a role where I could leverage all my experience and interests. A pure business role felt like much too far a deviation from the previous seven years I spent with Stikeman Elliott LLP, which I had thoroughly enjoyed. I had spent a lot of time building relationships and goodwill at Stikeman and felt that this would be hard to replicate somewhere new. Transactional work has high highs and low lows, but it keeps your daily work exciting. I wanted to make sure I would be equally challenged and energized by any new role I would take on, but was willing to sacrifice the ups and downs and unpredictability of transactional life.

With that in mind, I took a new direction, entering the field of legal technology. It was one of the best decisions I ever made. My new position has been just as challenging as my previous one.

Jevons "Legal" Paradox

In Chapter 2, we introduced the Jevons paradox, the idea that when a resource is delivered more efficiently, the consumption of that resource will actually increase (not decrease, as anticipated). In the legal field, the Jevons paradox means that as AI and other technologies make the delivery of legal services more efficient, that efficiency will drive more legal work—in the same way that more efficient refrigeration enabled an explosion of economic activity around frozen and refrigerated foods, not to mention more building of refrigerators themselves.

The Jevons paradox manifests itself in the legal space through more people doing legal work—work that never would have happened if not for greater efficiency. As technology enables more efficient delivery of services that were previously based on manual and unscalable processes, access to and use of those new forms of delivery will increase. We have already seen a dramatic increase in new legal jobs for people applying those technologies. We are also witnessing restructuring of the industry itself, creating new opportunities for people with a wider range of skills.

In this chapter, we'll show how AI and other technologies are creating *new jobs* and *new employers* in the legal space, and how those new roles require *new skill sets and new ways of thinking*—for both lawyers and other professionals in the industry.

A Growing Array of Legal Jobs

The primary job in the legal services industry has been the licensed lawyer or attorney. These professionals have typically been engaged in roles in the following broad categories:

- Private practice attorneys in law firms, including sole practitioners.
- Corporate lawyers, on in-house legal teams in corporations.
- Lawyers engaged in representing parties in the justice system: prosecutors, public defenders.
- Lawyers engaged in public policy: advisors to legislatures, regional and local governments, government agencies, public officials, and transnational and nongovernmental organizations.
- Judges, arbitrators, and other roles involved in adjudicating disputes.

Supporting lawyers in these roles are a few categories of professionals:

- *Paralegals, law clerks, legal secretaries.* Many of these have extensive knowledge of the law but they are not licensed to practice law.
- *Support staff.* This is made up of individuals that handle the support functions, most of which are typical in any business or organization, such as administrators, marketers, and IT staff.

These roles have remained fairly static for decades. However, with the introduction of technology to the industry, there has been an explosion of new roles involved in the delivery of legal services. Some of these roles still require the knowledge and expertise of a licensed lawyer, many require completely different skill sets, and others require a mix of legal and other skills. The newly added jobs engaged in the delivery of law fall into several broad categories including:

- *Jevons paradox jobs.* These are jobs being created by more efficient legal work. One might assume that technology would kill many of these jobs (like traditional associate roles). In fact, such jobs will very likely continue to grow largely because the more efficient delivery of legal services will generate greater demand for the work of lawyers.

- *Jobs driven by the increased use of legal data.* These include all kinds of data analyst roles—people who manage data and can extract meaningful and actionable insight from such data about legal transactions. This includes court-generated data, patent and other intellectual property data, data from public financial records, billing and pricing invoices, and data from case management systems.

- *Legal knowledge engineering roles directly involved in automating legal work.* This includes lawyers and others who train machine learning models to extract data from contracts, court decisions, dockets, and other legal data; lawyers who capture legal processes in expert systems and document automation systems; and other roles where lawyers are embedding legal knowledge into systems and processes in order to automate aspects of legal work.

- *Knowledge management roles.* This includes roles involved in capturing and distributing an organization's knowledge and expertise in order to leverage it.

- *Legal product management jobs.* Legal tech companies package legal services in products. Increasingly, this includes law firms and other organizations that embed their employees' expertise into customer-facing products. Products, including productized forms of legal services delivery, are better built with the expertise of product managers.

- *Innovation and strategy roles.* As legal organizations have turned to technology and new business models to support their delivery of legal services, new jobs have emerged for people capable of driving and supporting innovation, providing change management, and staking out a strategic direction.

- *Training and customer success roles.* Legal tech vendors, law firms, and in-house legal departments have all started to recognize the value of a customer-centric approach to service delivery. This has led to roles that ensure customers are getting the most out of legal offerings.

Legal Operations and CLOC

Legal operations is a broad term for a wide range of roles that entail the management of technology, people, and processes in the legal industry. To be effective, legal operations leaders must engage in various areas such as setting budgets, selecting priorities, and managing people and technology.

The Corporate Legal Operations Consortium (CLOC) is an association of in-house legal operations professionals that has grown rapidly in recent years from just a few dozen members in early 2016 to over 2,400 members today. This growth runs parallel to the growth of legal technology, and illustrates the need to fill new roles in legal operations. With that in mind, CLOC designed a useful model for describing the various functions that fit under the "Legal Ops" umbrella. The CLOC Core 12 model (see Figure 4.1) captures the scope of roles engaged in work around the delivery of legal services.

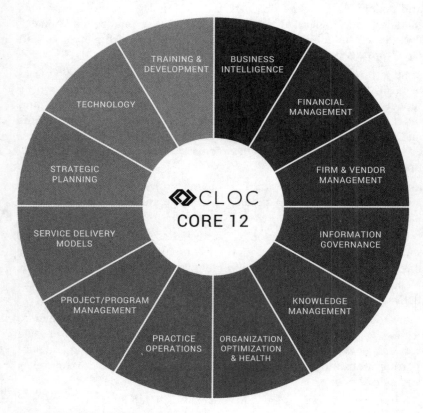

FIGURE 4.1 The CLOC Core 12.

Source: From Cloc, The CLOC Core 12, © 2020 Corporate Legal Operations Consortium, Inc.

The striking thing about the CLOC Core 12 is that these are all well-developed roles in other industries such as financial services and manufacturing, but are fairly new in legal. The growth of these roles is directly related to the impact of technology on legal practice. Lawyers are increasingly taking on leadership roles in these categories. The combination of an understanding of legal principles and processes with other business or technical skills is driving opportunity.

BYOT: BUILDING YOUR OWN TEAM

By Mary O'Carroll, Director of Legal Operations at Google and President of CLOC

I took the role of director of Legal Operations at Google in 2008, at a time when the company was experiencing rapid growth. Tackling operational challenges one by one, we've built a legal operations organization that's grown to accommodate many roles. Like many other Legal Operations teams, we oversee outside counsel management; pricing and financial management; vendor management; and "right sourcing" (which means figuring out how to match the value of the work with the right resource, whether it is internal, external, outside counsel, alternative legal service provider, or automation). Legal Operations organizations also manage the strategic planning, program management, professional development, and training for their lawyers; technology development and implementations, systems and tools, and knowledge management; data analytics; and so much more. Legal Operations teams aim to multiply their department's impact by driving innovation, operational excellence, and focused execution.

Today, you can do so much more than ever before. For example, you can scale your department a lot faster. This is one of the benefits of having new tools at your disposal that can help you handle what has become an explosion of data. In-house corporate legal departments have a lot more to work with than ever before. For decades, in-house teams did not have the systems or tools to capture and analyze data for things like outside counsel spending, which meant we had to turn to our law firms for everything. And, in some cases, they still used age-old processes. On top of that, the business model of almost all North American law firms continues to be based on the billable hour. This does not align well with client interests. Clients want innovation, value, and results. I've spoken with many tech providers who have pitched law firms saying they can do the work faster and cheaper, to which senior partners would respond with things like, "Why do things faster? Research is one of my most profitable areas."

There was not much demand for technology from law firms for decades. I believe that a large catalyst and driver of the demand for technology in the legal industry today has been the explosion of legal operations and desire to improve efficiency and effectiveness within corporations. Suddenly, you have people whose full-time roles are focused on doing things better and faster, and looking at innovative ways to get results. You now have so many possible, and effective, work scenarios and delivery options. We call this "right sourcing," and it is a large part of our roles. To optimize the value of your department, you need to figure out what should be done by humans, what can be automated, and where humans can work with automation. There are also things that you can stop doing altogether. All of this is entirely new. Not long ago, most legal issues would be sent directly to your law firm. You only had one option. Today, it is our responsibility to determine when to use each of the several options mentioned above. Sometimes that means sending the work to your firm, sometimes keeping it in-house, sometimes working together with a law firm or other legal services provider. For example, you can do data discovery and review with AI, and then use outside counsel to do a more thorough analysis of the most relevant data.

One result of this disaggregation of work is the increasing need for legal project managers who can bring all the moving pieces and parties together by using the three key components: people, process, and technology.

Change management has also become a big part of the process. You've got to have individuals skilled in change management who can step back, look at the situation, and ask the basic questions that lead to change:

- How is this currently being done today?
- Is this the best way?
- Is there a better way to do it?
- What is that better way?
- How can we make the necessary changes?
- What tools can we leverage?
- What changes can we leverage from a people perspective? A training perspective? A process standpoint?
- Can we consolidate some of the work, so we centralize it?
- Are the key people supportive of the change?
- Can they sell it to all those involved?

We have to ask ourselves questions like these as we develop and maintain a change management framework. Change is constant in today's business environment. This means the ability to address and manage change is essential.

Driving the New Jobs—Part 1: A New Legal Tech Sector

Where did all the new jobs described above come from? They didn't arise in a vacuum; they arose because of the development of technologies sold to law firms and legal departments by technology vendors. While some law firms and in-house legal departments have developed their own technology-based solutions to enhance the way they deliver legal services, the real driver of change and of these new jobs is an independent legal technology industry that has developed and blossomed in recent years.

The companies in that industry are creating tools that give lawyers new capabilities. As a result, previously unknown jobs have been created for people who learn how to effectively apply these new tools in service delivery.

There are many examples of this phenomenon in other industries and professions. Consider, for example, the field of marketing. Technology, especially the growth of the internet, has completely transformed the work that marketers do and the ways in which marketing services are delivered. At the same time, an entire ecosystem of marketing technology (*martech*) companies has developed in a few short years. The Martech 5000, a database of martech firms, is summarized in the chart in Figure 4.2.

This market has exploded, from 947 solutions offered in 2014 to over 8,000 in 2020. Each of these solutions represents a company providing marketing-related technology, in specialties such as content management, e-commerce and sales, and advertising and promotions.

FIGURE 4.2   The Martech 5000.

Source: Data from Chief MarTech

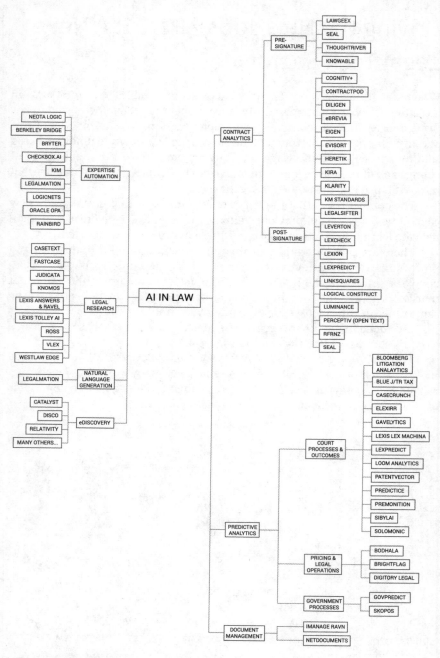

FIGURE 4.3 AI in law today.

Source: Courtesy of Michael Mills

Each of those new technologies creates new roles for the people who master them. Entire classes of jobs with names like growth hacker, marketing operations specialist, SEO specialist, and video marketer have gone from non-existent to becoming familiar titles in the marketing industry.

In addition, each of those companies employs anywhere from tens to thousands of people. Some of those people have traditional marketing backgrounds, others are primarily technologists, and an increasing number of them have interesting hybrid careers that straddle both tech and marketing. Some are even in-house lawyers. The same phenomenon is now occurring in the legal industry. The result of the application of technology to legal practice has created an entire legal tech sector, with hundreds of companies attracting millions in investment dollars. See Figure 4.3.

Investments in legal tech companies exceeded $1 billion in both 2018 and 2019, up from what was then considered a banner year of $150 million invested in 2013. The startup database Crunchbase identifies over a thousand young legal tech companies that have received some level of investment funding. Even just looking at the legal tech companies that leverage AI in their solutions, the companies active in the space are varied and growing.

As in the martech example, the availability of these tools has created entirely new roles in law firms, including legal knowledge engineers, data analysts, document automation specialists, and so forth. Martech created entirely new jobs and that's now happening in law firms.

Note the diversity of applications for AI in legal. AI touches litigation, transactional, restructuring, and tax practice. It leverages data from document production requests, contracts, corporate databases, and court records. Techniques used include expert systems, machine learning, and predictive analytics.

In addition to the jobs created for people who use these tools in law firms and legal departments, all of these companies—and many others offering non-AI applications in other fields like practice management, e-billing, case management, and knowledge management—have created jobs for lawyers, as well as technologists and other allied professionals.

AMPLIFYING LEGAL EXPERTISE AS A FULL-TIME JOB

By Corinne Geller, Director of Legal Knowledge Engineering, Kira Systems

As I mentioned at the start of the chapter, I made a career move from private practice to a legal tech job. In my position as director of Legal Knowledge Engineering at Kira Systems, I lead the company's legal knowledge engineering team by providing strategic direction in alignment with company mission, vision, and strategy. My goal is to encourage an environment where my team can develop their knowledge areas in order to maximize value for our users and for the company.

The Legal Knowledge Engineering team is composed of former lawyers, a paralegal, and a law librarian. Today, we're 13 full-time team members, joined by a bunch of contractors. We serve many purposes within the company, including: (i) teaching Kira concepts so that it can find similar concepts on new documents; (ii) prioritizing what Kira should learn by tracking changes in laws that would require new concepts to be found, and speaking with customers to figure out trends in the data that illustrate what the majority of customers would want to find; and (iii) helping to educate people both internally and externally as to how they can best use Kira. Based on the fact that we are former practicing lawyers, we can empathize with our customers when it comes to understanding their needs.

Additionally, I support our go-to-market teams (sales, customer value, marketing) as needed to facilitate awareness and usage of the built-in knowledge areas. I seek to maintain a high level of internal knowledge and awareness about our various industry applications and common use cases. And finally, I collaborate with our machine learning researchers, product managers, and designers to support the development of software features and roadmaps, helping ensure we are offering holistic solutions for our customers.

For me, private practice was not a sustainable life choice. My new job has provided me with a wonderful way to maintain a challenging and stimulating professional role, while still having the time to be connected and heavily involved in my child's home life. Private practice also sent me on a very linear career path—either stick it out to make partner at a law firm or transition to an in-house position. I believe my career path now has nearly infinite possibilities.

HOW AI HELPED A VISUALLY IMPAIRED LAWYER ACHIEVE HIS POTENTIAL

By Amar Jain, Associate at Cyril Amarchand Mangaldas

As a lawyer with complete blindness, I long faced challenges in my job, which became harder to perform owing to the inaccessibility of documents. I can think and communicate; I just "read" differently than others. My job is a text-heavy one. I have to consume large volumes of documents. The problem is that it was often hard to get them in a machine-readable form for my screen-reading software, and I had to spend lots of time with the documents to get to the parts that matter. Happily, AI has changed that for me. It helps me do my job to the fullest of my ability. This means others realize I *can* do this work just like everyone else.

In 2016, I joined Cyril Amarchand Mangaldas' (CAM) Mumbai office as a Capital Markets associate. In this role, I'm involved with due diligence, drafting and reviewing documents, commenting and negotiating, and managing work-flows. CAM—which many regard as the finest firm in India—tries to be "ahead of the curve," including when it comes to applying technology to legal practice. I have benefited from this greatly. I truly feel that I have a platform that enables me to do my tasks easily without assistance and with reasonable accommodations.

I discovered Kira at CAM and, quite honestly, it has created a world of possibility and opportunity for me. The nature of my job is to work with all kinds of documents. Reading printed documents is not possible for me owing to my visual impairment. And even if I get scanned documents, many of them are difficult to read for me because of poor scanning resolution, watermarks, headers and footers, or security settings. All of these make it very challenging to extract machine-readable text from them. To get the basic information I need, I typically had to print, rescan, and then OCR these documents. This was extremely time-consuming and cumbersome. Then I got Kira, which works on these documents faster than all the existing technologies. A review of two to three thousand documents that would typically take me a week to complete could be accomplished within a day with Kira. Not only does Kira automate a lot of the work around this process, it also helps direct me to the information I need. This removes the barrier of my firm needing to make a request to provide machine readable documents for me specifically, which often required complicated client requests, which confronts them with the confidentiality and security risks.

There's the speed in which Kira helps, but there's also the accuracy. On some documents, it was very difficult for me to find information I needed. Party names and dates could be tricky to spot, stamps could be indiscernible, and handwriting mixed with text caused problems. Now, I get documents that have already been reviewed by our innovation team based on what Kira has extracted. Removing the worry of my ability to process the information and maintain the level of accuracy we need to do effective work gives me great confidence.

Just a few years ago, I wouldn't have been able to do capital markets due diligence work as effectively as I can today. It was practically impossible to do the work at the optimal level of speed and accuracy that we're now at. AI Solutions like Kira have not only impacted how people perceive me within my firm and industry, they've positively impacted my career progression and outlook. For someone like me, who wasn't able to perform to the best of his ability because of accessibility barriers or unreadable documents, AI has changed the game. The ability to work as quickly and efficiently as my fellow colleagues gives me a true sense of equality.

My managing partner, Mr. Cyril Shroff, says, "Amar is a brave and gifted lawyer. He has never let his challenges come in the way of his contributions. He has a sharp memory and his other senses have compensated in abundance. We are delighted that our adoption of Kira has had a positive impact on his life. We pride ourselves on our diversity and innovation mindset. And this is a shining example."

Unfortunately, the majority of today's business software remains inaccessible for visually impaired people. Laws like Section 508 of the US Rehabilitation Act of 1973 are certainly moving things in the right direction, but—broadly speaking—business software is not designed with accessibility in mind. I look forward to more and more advancement in AI, including accessibility improvements. It really helps people like me to be our best.

Driving the New Jobs—Part 2: New Tech-Enabled Business Models

Another sector of the legal industry that is creating new legal jobs is the Alternative Legal Service Provider (ALSP) sector, also sometimes referred to as NewLaw or Law Companies. These are not traditional law firms but they perform many of the functions that traditional firms have offered including Litigation and Investigation Support, Legal Research, Document Review, eDiscovery, and Regulatory Risk and Compliance.

Some ALSPs are staffing operations, providing a flexible workforce for large-scale projects. Others are in-sourcing operations, providing lawyers who serve as subject matter experts on a temporary basis.

Increasingly, however, ALSPs are tackling large-scale process work with a combination of technology and process management techniques. Many of these operations have the focus and capabilities to deliver AI-enabled services at scale, and require many of the same legal operations skills that are driving legal operations at law firms and in-house legal departments.

A 2019 study of the ALSP market by Thomson Reuters showed that total revenue among these employers was $10.7 billion, and that they had experienced compounded annual growth of 12.9% over the previous two years.[1]

There are a number of large independent ALSPs, including: Elevate, Factor (formerly Axiom), Integreon, and UnitedLex. The Big Four accounting and audit firms (PwC, EY, KPMG, and Deloitte) also have legal arms and are expanding into the legal space. These players are global and they work at scale. Just as an example, PwC Legal has 3,500 lawyers working in 90 countries (not including PwC's own in-house lawyers). Consistent with their work in tax, compliance, and other corporate advisory work, the Big Four are focused not so much on practicing law (in fact, in the US they are prohibited from practicing) as on building out processes and technology to handle parts of the corporate legal workflow that can be automated.

The appearance of these new types of legal services providers to the legal market has, like the growth of pure legal technology companies, generated entirely new types of roles for people who combine legal skills and experience with process and technology skills.

A BIG FOUR PERSPECTIVE ON #NEWLAW

By Mark Ross, Principal at Deloitte Tax LLP—Legal Business Services

The legal profession today is vastly different from the artisanal profession of the past. At Deloitte Tax LLP ("Deloitte"), we view it through the lens of business—the business of law. Over the next 5–10 years, we will see a period of increasing technological and operating model innovations driving transformation in the delivery to and consumption of services by the corporate legal department.

Corporate legal departments are contending with a multitude of interrelated and overlapping market forces: The volume of work continues to increase exponentially as organizations deal with an explosion in data, rapid changes in regulations, and an increasingly interconnected global marketplace. In-house teams lack the bandwidth to keep pace. Additionally, most are trained in the practice of law, not the business of delivering legal services. All the while, the corporate legal department is not only being asked to do more with less but also to go a step further and partner with business to drive value.

The opportunity for legal departments to benefit from AI is immense, with a multitude of potential use cases. In the contracting function, automated, intelligent intake and triage driving delegation to alternative resources or self-help frees up in-house attorneys' time to work on more strategic matters. By thinking beyond the four corners of the contract and linking auto-extracted contractual data to data in finance, ERP, and CRM systems, organizations can monitor and realize contractual performance. Asking the following questions can help them ensure that obligations and milestones are appropriately addressed and that discounts and other financial incentives are identified and realized:

- Where should corporate legal departments start?
- With so many choices, what tool is right for them?
- How do they enhance the value of legacy systems and connect them to new systems?
- How should they identify meaningful business insights and metrics from a mass of data?

The challenge is not one of system and tool functionality but, rather, one of selection, implementation, and change management.

To help solve it, we at Deloitte are strategically investing in both external and internal talent, with the ambition to improve the experience and benefits for our clients. Transformation of the legal function requires multidisciplinary approaches that embrace process standardization, automation and AI, global delivery, alternative resource models, and continuous improvement. The talent to deliver on that approach includes knowledge engineers, technologists, process analysts, management consultants, procurement and sourcing specialists, data scientists, and, of course, some with legally trained backgrounds.

Prior to joining Deloitte, I spent the last 15 years working for boutique alternative legal services providers. The most compelling reason for me joining Deloitte is that for legal business services, we are able to provide a singular destination for the corporate legal buyer. Deloitte has size and scale, diversity of talent and experience, business reputation, technological advancement, leadership knowledge, and transformation and change management capabilities. These capabilities make us distinctly advantaged to respond to the evolving circumstances of the corporate legal department.

New and Better Jobs: Diverse Skill Sets Needed

It's not hard to see that lawyers and others with skills relevant to the legal services industry have, in a few short years, been presented with a much wider field of play for their services. Along with traditional law firms and in-house corporate legal departments, legal tech companies have created new roles for people who understand how to apply the new tools to legal service delivery. Those companies have also become an attractive market for lawyers with a technology bent. Many founders of legal tech companies, such as Noah, are former lawyers who have built companies around problems and challenges they encountered in private practice, and new roles for lawyers are common in that sector. Former Slaughter & May associates Chris Millerchip and Rob Dow founded Practical Law Company back in the early 1990s, and exited to Thomson Reuters in 2013 for a vast amount of money. Alma Asay, a former litigation associate at Gibson, Dunn & Crutcher, founded Allegory Law, a litigation management platform that was acquired by Integreon. Haley Altman was a corporate and securities law partner at Ice Miller before leveraging that experience into a transaction management platform company, Doxly, which was sold to Litera in 2019. There are a lot more examples.

The ALSP / NewLaw market has been one of the fastest-growing segments in the legal tech industry. These companies present many employment opportunities for lawyers with business process and technology skills.

However, many of these new jobs require a wider set of skills than most lawyers have obtained in law school and/or in private practice. The broadening of skill sets and multidisciplinary training and education are another area of legal employment growth.

AI and other technologies are also expanding the legal job market by simply making it a more interesting place to work. Until recently, career paths in law were quite limited and were often characterized by routine work, inefficiencies, and a very limited move "up or out" career path.

The new jobs we mention above, and new types of employers, require people with new skill sets. The legal profession is on the verge of a transformation in how lawyers see themselves and their roles. Technology and new business models are driving that change.

The introduction of technology into the legal services industry has brought an increasing focus on *how* legal services are delivered. Technology enables legal services organizations to even change the way they package and price their services. The growth of all those new roles and changes in legal services requires a more multidisciplinary approach to talent development in the industry.

The Delta Lawyer Competency Model

Today, with the changing landscape of the legal industry, lawyers are being asked to acquire skills beyond the traditional subject-matter expertise they acquire in law school.

A small working team of academics and analysts focused on lawyer skills has developed the Delta Model, designed to illustrate the three areas of competency necessary for the modern lawyer to be most successful. The team included Natalie Runyon of Thomson Reuters, Alyson Carrel of Northwestern Pritzker School of Law, Cat Moon of Vanderbilt Law School, Shellie Reid of the Access to Justice Tech Fellows Program, and Gabe Teninbaum of Suffolk University Law School.[2]

The team designed a model that illustrated the three major components of a modern lawyer's skill set illustrated as a delta (triangle) shape, as shown in Figure 4.4. Each side of the Delta Model represents one broad skill set:

- *Legal skills.* These are the traditional subject-matter expertise in law that lawyers acquire in law school.
- *Business and operations skills.* These are the skills that enable lawyers to see their work as part of an ongoing business, which includes knowledge of technology, process management, data analytics, and so forth.
- *Personal effectiveness skills.* These include empathy, communication, and relationship management skills that lawyers need to be able to effectively carry out the cross-disciplinary work inside and outside their organizations.

DELTA MODEL V.3

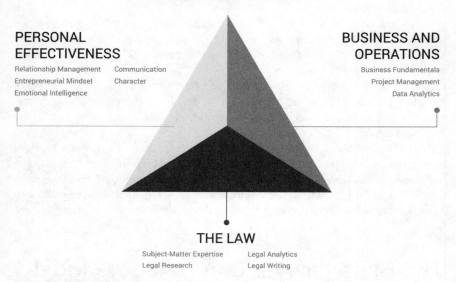

PERSONAL EFFECTIVENESS

Relationship Management   Communication
Entrepreneurial Mindset   Character
Emotional Intelligence

BUSINESS AND OPERATIONS

Business Fundamentals
Project Management
Data Analytics

THE LAW

Subject-Matter Expertise   Legal Analytics
Legal Research   Legal Writing

FIGURE 4.4   The Delta Lawyer Competency Model.

Source: Reprinted with permission from Thomson Reuters Legal Executive Institute. Copyright 2020. All Rights Reserved.

A key aspect of the Delta Model is its flexibility. There is no set ratio of the skills prescribed that all lawyers need to acquire; some lawyers will have more skills on one side of the delta, depending on their roles. But the model proposes that every role in the legal services industry includes some mix of these skills, with many roles requiring that one skill be more dominant than the others in the makeup of the individual. It's generally been well understood that different skill sets exist in law practice, but as more new roles are introduced, the ratio of skill sets will naturally vary to an even greater degree.

Figure 4.5 models the relevant importance of the three sides of the delta to four different types of legal jobs:

- A law firm partner.
- A legal solutions architect.
- A lawyer with strong brief-writing and research skills.
- A manager or team leader.

Different people in the industry will have different ratios of these three skill sets depending on their backgrounds and the type of law they practice.

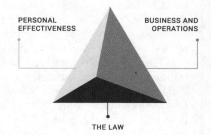

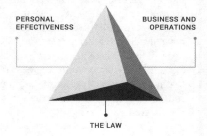

FIGURE 4.5   Predominant competencies.

LOOK FOR BALANCED THINKERS

By Jason Barnwell, Assistant General Counsel—Modern Legal at Microsoft

I lead Microsoft's Modern CELA team within the Office of the General Counsel of Microsoft's Corporate, External, and Legal Affairs department. Our mandate is to bring industry-leading innovation to how we work at Microsoft, highlighting and showcasing how Microsoft technologies make us more effective, efficient, and capable. Modern CELA applies a multidisciplinary approach to serve a multidisciplinary organization that operates at the intersection of law, technology, and policy. And my practice evolved from convergence of two vocations that require very different ways of thinking.

My undergraduate engineering degree experiences still shape my "modern legal" perspective and skill set with a common approach to problem solving. First, I learned how to take big problems and break them into small problems.

Second, I learned that there is a manual for almost everything. It could be a book, it could be a video, but somewhere there is some documentation that explains someone else's approach upon which I can build. Finally, our instructors' ability to meet me where I was varied, and I needed to be able to teach myself.

This problem-solving approach focuses on looking for patterns. The training shifts your mindset. If something looks unique, step back until it looks like something you have seen before. The patterns and the cycles eventually connect and reveal how things interact as a system. Most complex problems are systems problems that require solution approaches that address the bigger picture.

Conventional law school instruction focuses on critical thinking. If things look similar, keep taking a step forward until they look different. This is how you distinguish situations that seem similar. It is immensely valuable. A lawyer's lawyer perceives the smallest details in fact and law to fashion outcomes-focused arguments that influence decisions.

I see people struggle to balance the critical thinking that says, "These have small differences; let's treat them differently," with systems thinking that says, "These have small differences; let's treat them the same." Our innovation capacity is reduced when we get stuck in one of these modes and lose the ability to change perspective, apply judgment to resolve the discord, and find the best solutions. It manifests in many ways.

A frequent innovation-focused conversation with attorneys starts off discussing how their work might be done differently using common patterns or tools and often produces, "Oh, but you don't understand. What I do here is different every time. It is not reducible to any of these more generalized models." They will then tell you why a pattern approach is appropriate for some other legal work outside their practice, which they regard as too complex. The building blocks of most legal practices reveal repetition with patterns. This does not mean the work is not complex. It means the experts can benefit from assistance that eases their process burdens.

We optimize work by adding process and technology to the parts that make sense. Many legal professionals presume process and automation must cover every scenario they might see. They then consider how challenging that would be, and dismiss the idea that there might be substantial value in focusing on the 80% of the work that reflects known patterns. This automatable portion is usually the work they enjoy the least, because it requires less critical thinking. But identifying opportunities to transform their practice requires reflecting on the work as a system and recognizing the parts that have patterns that are materially similar, despite the deviations. This is a teachable skill.

When legal professionals acquire design thinking capabilities they learn how to reengineer their work to focus on the parts of their practice that require human cognition strengths (empathy, context, and judgment). And we can augment optimized practices with technical capabilities to deliver even more value. Bringing the practice design skill set closer to the subject matter expert produces more ideas, better ideas, and solutions better tailored to serve the underlying job-to-be-done. The people who invest to bring subject matter expertise and practice design together will have more opportunities because they will be able to manufacture them. They will also create a practice that constantly adapts and evolves because the design process requires critique of how we practice. A growth mindset is a key feature of a work culture that stresses learning and adaptability.

We want people who can balance their thinking and find practical results. We want to bring in people who understand when to move in close and when to step back. Practitioners may believe an operations mindset that seeks to reduce actions to a process diminishes our work. Some of the most brilliant minds in history saw the elegance of patterns in things that others regarded as inconceivably complex. It is the highest form of our art to reduce the elements of a legal issue that truly impact outcomes, and to create models that explain our analysis. When we successfully apply processes to patterns, we find ways to scale.

This is a mindset. It starts with curiosity and presumes that if we examine issues from enough directions and with the right perspective, we can see what makes a situation special and how it maps to patterns. I lucked into this approach by moving from engineering to law, but attorneys with all backgrounds can learn more about design thinking, systems thinking, and lean process improvement to evolve their practices. They are the core building blocks of many disciplines that focus on delivering repeatable excellence at scale. Legal professionals who embrace these complementary skills will be better prepared to thrive in a future that may see increasing levels of volatility, uncertainty, complexity, and ambiguity because they will constantly be positioned to evolve and deliver more value.

Conclusion

Legal technology, and AI specifically, are drivers of much of the growth in the legal industry today, including job creation. It's common for most lawyers to speculate about the extent to which AI is *taking away* from their roles by automating some tasks and shifting some of their work to technology or other types of legal services providers. A common response to that line of thinking is that AI allows lawyers to eliminate routine and lower-value tasks from their daily workflow, allowing them to focus more attention on the important stuff such as advising clients, understanding their challenges, finding new solutions, and providing higher-quality service.

The real effect of AI, however, is bigger than that; AI is actually generating more opportunities. As the Jevons paradox shows, more efficient delivery of a valuable resource like legal advice and services results in greater consumption. Such growth requires lawyers to consider the impact of AI not just on their current roles, but on all the dynamic new parts of the legal industry that technology has enabled.

Notes

1. Alternative legal service providers in 2019. https://www.legalexecutiveinstitute. com/wp-content/uploads/2019/06/ALSP-infographic.jpg
2. Runyon, N., A. Carrel, C. Moon, S. Reid, and G. Teninbaum. 2019. The Delta Model: Simple, accurate, versatile (125). Legal Evolution (November 10). https://www .legalevolution.org/2019/11/the-delta-model-simple-accurate-versatile-125/

CHAPTER 5

Amplifying Legal Expertise

From One-to-One Advisory to Scalable, One-to-Many Service Delivery

A few years ago, a very highly respected, well-versed senior partner in a niche practice at a major law firm decided it was time to retire.* He had put in nearly 40 years and thought it was the right time to move on with his life. Not only would his colleagues miss him personally, but they knew that they would also miss his accumulated wisdom in his specialty area. He was, in essence, a "go-to" guy when it came to answering tough questions and providing sage legal advice.

The firm had recently been tinkering with its new contract analysis software (Kira) and brainstormed with the partners in the group ways that they could use the tool for knowledge transfer. The idea was that rather than using traditional knowledge transfer methods, which would have provided a general, static overview of his insights, they would use artificial intelligence to train models that would assist junior attorneys while they worked on similar transactions.

Since the senior partner was not particularly technically savvy, the firm assigned a lawyer from its knowledge management team to work with the partner to capture his expertise—specifically, his knowledge of complex agreements for certain types of transactions. The partner and knowledge management attorney spent many hours walking through examples of agreements and the terms therein, mapping them to concepts that the KM

----

*This true story was told to us by Amy Monaghan, Senior Practice Innovations Manager at Perkins Coie. The story was from another firm.

attorney ultimately used to capture his knowledge in an artificial intelligence system. Sometimes the partner would join her in her office and she would show him how she was transferring his knowledge into models that others would be able to draw on. After several months, the KM attorney had trained dozens of models that were able to recognize language in these complex agreements. The task was complete, and ironically, the partner said, "That's it?" as if it was supposed to be more complicated—after all, it was state-of-the-art technology. And yet, despite the ease of the process, the finished product of this lengthy procedure seemed like something out of science fiction. It was, however, the new reality of how AI can amplify legal expertise.

Amplification: What Lawyers Can Learn from Rock Stars

Amplifying expertise has taken many forms over the years, including templates, books, white papers, journal articles, blogs, courses, seminars, speaking engagements, webinars, podcasts, and social media posts. Clearly, there are many ways in which we can inform, enlighten, and teach other people based on our areas of expertise.

However, these forms of amplification are limited in that they are not interactive. You can read a book, blog, or journal article but you cannot directly ask questions, or see the methods described applied to new scenarios. You can ask a question at a seminar or webinar, but you can only get the data as provided by the host or speaker, and a given speaker can only be in one seminar at a time. AI presents the opportunity to do both, provide static information, but also to interact by answering new questions, or applying methods to new data. Even better, it scales; no longer are you limited by the time of a single domain expert. If their knowledge and behavior are encoded into an AI, you can have as many copies of that AI working at the same time as you want.

Beyond law firms, corporate legal departments can also now meet the needs of other internal departments promptly, providing guidance and solutions to legal questions from marketing, finance, HR, and operations teams on a daily basis. For example, imagine if you could analyze the license of software you are looking to buy to get an initial assessment about compliance issues without needing to involve your compliance team. With an AI that has learned to recognize risk by watching your compliance team, you could actually do this. Or consider the recent global pandemic. It caused many corporations to need to quickly look at the force majeure clauses in their contracts.

With AI, this task can take mere minutes, but without AI, it could involve days, weeks, or months of costly lawyer time.

One of the most interesting implications of artificial intelligence is that if you teach it to be like you, to answer questions as you would, or to make the legal decisions that you would make in a specific situation, you could—effectively—be doing work when you're not actually doing work. Consequently, the retiring senior partner mentioned above could be vacationing in the Cayman Islands while his insights are benefiting attorneys in his former firm. If this sounds closely like a "robotic" attorney, it is, minus the tailored suits and cliché stock photos.

Another way to think about amplification is through a comparison to music. We're not referring to turning up the volume to 11. Rather, 150 years ago, if you felt like listening to music, you needed to figure out a live option. Maybe you could get your wife to play the flute while your son sang and your daughter played the piano. Or a wandering musical troupe might happen by. Or you could go see a show. Now, you have *many* options to listen to a vast array of songs and performers, instantly. This is because we can now record and distribute music. We are all better off for being able to listen to music on demand. But artists are also much better off in this world. Before, they could only make money while actually performing. Today, they can record a track, and—if people listen to it—make money while they sleep, lie on the beach, or smash up a posh L.A. hotel room. So, what of lawyers? While some create and sell books, templates, and other general-purpose content, a hit NDA form does not appear to be the same path to riches as a chart-topping song. This is because legal work is so context-specific. It needs lawyers to consider the facts and circumstances of the situation. This makes lawyers like pre-gramophone musicians, only making money through actually working.

AI offers lawyers the opportunity to change this. Law is context specific, but AI can enable lawyers to teach an AI how to respond in various situations, and then sit back while it works. Once, Noah labored for months teaching Kira how to find change of control clauses. Now, years and years later, junior associates at a majority of the world's most prestigious law firms have a virtual Noah working with them, day and night. (Alas, these days, Noah spend too much of his time doing new work like this book and not nearly enough on the beach; he is far from living the rock-star life.) This actually goes a step further than selling prerecorded music: technology now enables people to create content that's personalized. So if you feel like having Frank Sinatra sing a personalized "Happy Birthday to You" to your spouse, or perhaps having Notorious B.I.G., Neil Young, Beyonce, or another personal favorite sing the birthday song, you could do that, too. This is becoming possible in music.[1] And law is now following the beat of that music.

Amplifying en Masse

One inspiring part of practicing at a large firm for Noah was seeing how much force the firm could quickly bring to bear when it needed to. As Lehman Brothers collapsed, hundreds of his colleagues from different practice groups were instantly helping them. On a smaller scale, Noah remembers *really* needing to rapidly find a critical document in some paper-stuffed boxes, and getting a group of several summer associates on it right away.

Smaller firms have traditionally been relatively disadvantaged by their inability to scale up. Thanks to AI enhancement, mid-sized and even smaller firms can also now do larger projects (though maybe not the size of the Lehman debtor representation!). AI can take on tasks that would have previously required more available personnel than most firms have.

The Three Most Important Things about Training AI

Today, most legal AI learns to work by being trained. Training needs to be done well; this is very much a garbage-in, garbage-out situation. Since 2011 at Kira Systems, we have put lots of effort into teaching our AI how to find clauses in contracts. This is a major responsibility. We're well aware that even if it's the end of the workday in Canada, it may be the start of business in another part of the world, and if someone is using a model that we have trained, it's very important that it works properly. We know our users have high standards.

There are three keys to successfully amplifying learning through AI:

1. Know what you would like to teach the AI—be a subject matter expert, or work with one.
2. Get comfortable with your technology. Note that some AI systems can be simple to use and train, and they do not require much more technical expertise than having a basic comfort level with computers.
3. Be able to clearly communicate your ideas to AI, as it will emulate precisely what you teach it. An AI won't fix your mistakes or biases. While Noah found teaching AI almost fun, you don't necessarily have to do it yourself—you can have someone communicate it for you.

When determining who will be training your AI, it helps to find someone who is diligent, fastidious, and consistent. A partner Noah respects said that one way to distinguish the best lawyers from the rest of the pack is to seek out those who—when they're lying in bed at 2:00 a.m. and start to think of something that they screwed up—promptly get out of bed to fix it. They care that much about getting it right. This is equally true for people teaching AIs. Technology works best when training is precise. Often, you'll find that the people who are really good at the training process are perfectionists willing to go the extra mile.

MY EXPERIENCE BUILDING A TEAM OF AMPLIFIERS

By Anne McNulty, Senior Director of Customer Value, Kira Systems

Teaching a concept to an AI system means giving it real world examples to learn from. As the AI analyzes these examples, it looks for patterns that provide it with a framework for recognizing that same concept whenever it encounters it again. The system's ability to do this accurately depends on the sophistication of the technology itself and the quality of the training data provided. The more consistent the data and the more representative it is of a particular concept, the more accurate the system will be when its learning is applied.

When teaching an AI system, therefore, it helps to have individuals who are precise, disciplined, and methodical doing the work. Furthermore, if the task is quite technical—like identifying important language in legal documents—it is essential that those individuals also have a firm grasp of the subject matter and its practical applications. After all, it is their knowledge and experience that is being captured. The system will be only as proficient as its trainers.

In our experience, lawyers who have practiced for around four years at a top-tier law firm are best suited to doing this kind of work (at least in teaching our software to find data points in contracts). Lawyers with this level of experience have acquired significant know-how in their respective areas of expertise. They are also highly adept at analyzing a wide variety of contracts. At the same time, they haven't yet advanced to the point where they are expected to delegate more and more of this kind of analytical work in order to focus on relationship building. In other words, they are at a sweet spot in their career where their expertise and practical skills are perfectly suited to teaching the system effectively.

At Kira Systems, our Legal Knowledge Engineering (LKE) team consists of former practicing lawyers who possess all of the above attributes. Each of our LKE managers oversees one or more subject matter areas (e.g., real estate, banking, and finance) that we offer as part of Kira's built-in intelligence. These managers are all deeply knowledgeable about the types of contracts that lawyers practicing in these areas need to review. The LKE team also includes junior lawyers, who typically handle the initial stage of training under the supervision of one of the managers. This provides an excellent learning opportunity for them to gain an intimate understanding of the many ways in which a particular concept can appear in a contract. For example, once someone has seen 200 different ways a non-compete provision can be drafted in an employment agreement, it's hard to miss it. In this way, Kira's AI learns while facilitating its users' learning and development.

Let's Agree to Not Disagree

While you want a domain expert to train the system, there's not always an agreement over who the right domain expert is. Just as clients will argue over which firm is better at a specific area of law, internal disagreement in organizations and law firms is not unusual. You're likely to have a collection of alternative viewpoints.

In smaller firms or corporate law departments, a top expert and leading contender for training purposes can more easily stand out from the crowd than in a larger firm where half a dozen excellent M&A attorneys will all provide reasons why they should train the system. Often, the first question centers on defining what needs to be included in the training and what is extraneous. A senior person at a major law firm once professed that the most time-consuming part of training Kira was actually agreeing internally on what definitions they were using to train the system rather than the actual training itself.

While you may get lucky and have a collective agreement over who is considered the leading expert in a specific area, in other cases, you will have multiple experts involved in the training. This often results in a cooperative pre-training effort, whereby there is a resulting internal decision based on answering several questions, such as: What will the system be looking for? How does this benefit us and our clients now and in the future? How much time and how many resources can we put toward this training effort? After all, if all 10 attorneys in the legal department of a corporation are working on the training effort, who's fielding important legal inquiries from other departments?

One solution that is often presented is to dump in as much data as possible. This is based on the idea that more is better. The popular wisdom is that the more training data you pour into an AI, the smarter it gets. Therefore, if you pour all of these experts' knowledge together into one pool, you're going to end up with some type of super-intelligence. In reality, on more complicated or nuanced tasks, this is not always true. Data is important, yes, but not for the reasons people think. In particular, if dissenting opinions are poured in together, the system won't resolve the disagreements. It won't suddenly become smarter than all of the individual components. It will instead result in a very conflicted, diluted response that is—very possibly—worse. The system will get confused. If you poured every condiment in the kitchen into a recipe for more taste, it would be more difficult to taste anything. AI is similar; more training data isn't necessarily better.

Having to identify the best training data for a given subject area forces firms to address things that may have never been addressed before. For example, most firms don't stop to rethink the question "What is the firm's position on a particular issue?" Often, firms assume that everyone is on the same page. However, this is not always the case, and training AI can shed light on differences in the firm's stance on issues that will then need to be discussed.

With that in mind (disagreement) we did our own study in which we included a group of highly qualified lawyers and had them all do the exact same document review task.[2] We then looked at the results to see how often they agreed with one another and how often they disagreed. As it turned out, they only agreed with each other 70% of the time, which is a shockingly low number.

Another interesting part about that experiment was that we also trained our system to replicate the behavior of each person. When we measured how often the resulting individual AI systems disagreed with each other, it matched roughly what we saw in the humans, which was quite an interesting observation. It basically showed that we can capture individual human differences in knowledge. This means that based on the beliefs and attitudes of whoever is training the system, the results may differ, which takes us back to carefully selecting who will be providing the expertise and making sure they are clear on what they are trying to get the AI to learn.

Today, many companies are using innovation teams to help them execute their AI strategy. Such teams can take the lead when it comes to how to most effectively implement and train AI. A central authority can serve as an arbiter (or mediator) for disagreements over what to train. That said, sometimes it's best to just pick an individual perspective and go with it. There's no reason AI-using firms and companies can't also have multiple different "personal models" done.

Build Value for the Firm Itself

At one point in the television show *Mad Men,* several of the advertising executives decided to leave the agency and form their own competitive agency. The old agency—which had just been acquired for big money—was decimated. As in advertising, the key assets of law firms walk out the door every night (apart from when they have to pull all-nighters).

Top attorneys regularly lateral move to other firms (or start their own), bringing all their clients with them, and largely being able to practice the same type of law at their new firm as at their old firm. In some cases, they also bring their associates along. According to a 2019 ALM Intelligence study, firms are hiring to facilitate faster growth: Roughly $20.4 billion of client revenue has moved firms due to laterals between 2014 and 2018. Lateral partner hires represent the single largest source of revenue growth potential for law firms.

Legal AI (and other technology and process improvements) offer the opportunity to build value in the firm and its systems, instead of only its lawyers, making a law firm more than the sum of its people. This enhancement means lawyers can reach their fullest potential, practice their best law. It also means that they won't be as effective if they leave their firm. Think of Scottie Pippen and the Chicago Bulls dynasty in the 1990s, winning six NBA championships. Playing alongside Jordan, the greatest basketball player in the world, for a forward-thinking coach, Phil Jackson, who established the innovative "triangle" offense, and under management who surrounded their stars with the best possible role players, Pippen's game elevated to a level where he was a perennial All-Star. After the Bulls, Pippen went on to play with Houston and Portland, but he would never come close to that magic. He was still a decent player, but all of his stats declined and none of those teams had any meaningful playoff success. A high-value system increases the success potential of everyone involved.

For a law firm or corporate legal department, the use of technology to gather, maintain, and train lawyers in how they do things as an organization can help establish the organization as a unique entity. This also means that attorneys can't just go to another firm and necessarily be as successful.

Are There Limits to Amplifying?

As lawyers get more familiar with using and training AIs, they will need to consider how widely they are willing to share their captured expertise, and how to divide their time between practicing law and building AI models. Will they focus on leveraging their trained system for advantage in selling and delivering human-labor-based services, or will they instead turn into more product developers, intentionally spending their time training AI models that can then go off and work independently? In other words, will they opt for the status quo of today, augmented, or will they push to build a new business model, where they train an AI and then sit back and get paid while it does the work?

Will lawyers be willing to share models they build outside their firm? Our best guess is that it will depend. Most centrally, it will depend on whether there's demand. Are people willing to pay? If so, then how many and how much? As client service professionals, many lawyers are used to answering "yes" to meet client needs. We know lawyers who have skipped their own elaborate birthday celebrations to instead pull an all-nighter, taken calls before walking down the aisle to get married, or emailed from the delivery room bed about to give birth. It's hard to imagine many of them drawing the line at selling their encapsulated expertise if they believe this is in the best interests of their clients.

It will also depend on who is asking. Law firm lawyers seem very likely to share models with their clients, but less likely to share with their fiercest law firm competitors. That said, the vibrant International Legal Technology Association (fondly known as ILTA) stands as proof that otherwise-competitive law firms will heavily collaborate and share knowledge around technology.

Finally, it should depend on whether the law firm or company sees the material to be shared as the secret sauce of an area they dominate, or more of a commodity. We expect firms to focus more on protecting their crown jewels. So, for example, a firm with a world-leading aviation practice and middling other groups might be very willing to share AI content it built around M&A or employment law work, but be much more careful with its aviation models, especially if they are built on hard-to-get training data. Or, perhaps, the aviation leader would see releasing the aviation models as an opportunity to further demonstrate the firm's dominance. Or maybe the firm would find more revenue opportunities for releasing models where buyers would be most interested in having them.

As firms and companies share more and more of their expertise in the form of AI models, we may see a further homogenization of law firm quality. This is in line with a trend that has been happening for some time. For example, 40 years ago, few firms were experienced at M&A work, which left an opening for then-emerging firms like Skadden and Wachtell to build leading practices during the 1980s takeover boom. Now there might be 75 firms that can do standard M&A deals at a very respectable level. Over the past 25 years, new shaped and fat ski technology has made difficult, powdery slopes accessible to a much broader range of skiers. Similarly, AI (and other technology and process tools) should help bring more practitioners up to a "good enough" level. Of course, the flip is also true, where top lawyers can use their expertise to train better models than others, thus further fortifying their position.

THE EMERGENCE OF LEGALZOOM

By Eddie Hartman, Co-Founder of LegalZoom

We launched LegalZoom in September 2000 with a very specific problem in mind. We'd seen that the benefits of the law primarily went to the very small group of people who had quality legal representation; without a lawyer in your corner, the law often worked against you. By acting without legal help, most people lost what they thought was their birthright: equality before the law.

Our vision was that we could harness the vast power and reach of the internet to correct this imbalance. That's why our first tag line was "We put the law on your side."

Interest was low at first, and we questioned whether our little company would survive. However, by mid-2001, business was doubling every month. We had come up with a service that mattered to people.

Important Products

When you start a business like this, you're dealing with people's emotions. Writing a will involves thinking about your death and what you'll leave to the people you love. An entity formation is often a vehicle for someone's dreams, or a parachute for someone facing the loss of a job. Divorce, bankruptcy, and child custody battles are among the hardest life moments. Yet most authorities estimate that 80% of serious legal problems go unaddressed, if not more. That is a tragic statistic, not in the least because leaving so many out of our legal system weakens our collective confidence in the institution itself. Imagine a society where 80% of serious medical problems went unaddressed. It's unthinkable, yet it is a reasonable parallel to the legal crisis in America today.

We started out with a slate of 10 core products focused on common needs such as business formation, intellectual property protection, and estate planning. We later discovered that we could profitably offer legal plans at a shockingly affordable rate, enabling our customers to get quality legal help whenever they needed it. The upswell of interest following the 2008 financial crisis spurred us to bundle legal plans with our products, which continues to this day.

Through our legal plans, we offered access to actual lawyers who could provide specific legal advice. However, we were still limited in how we could work with lawyers, and therefore we were limited in how we could help our customers. We truly wanted to offer nothing short of full legal care to the people who came to us. So, the next step was actually acquiring a law firm, which LegalZoom did in late 2015.

Today I see LegalZoom's growth not only as a sign that we built a healthy business but also as a signal for the ongoing demand for greater access to justice for a vastly underserved public.

Amplifying Legal Expertise

In over 20 years, LegalZoom has served over 4 million customers, meeting a wide range of legal needs. While we are just part of the ecosystem of companies attacking the access to justice crisis, we are proud to have been among the pioneers.

Notes

1. Dhariwal, P., Heewoo Jun, and C. M. Payne. 2020. Jukebox. OpenAI.com (April 30). https://openai.com/blog/jukebox/
2. Roegiest, Adam, and Anne McNulty. 2019. Variations in assessor agreement in due diligence. Kira Systems (March). https://kirasystems.com/science/variations-assessor-agreement-due-diligence/.

CHAPTER 6

The Ethics of Lawyers Using— and Not Using—AI

As technology becomes a bigger and bigger part of our lives, its ethical implications get more attention. This extends from the positioning of security cameras, to anonymity online, to the training data used to teach machine learning algorithms. Unsurprisingly, it's also an issue around legal AI. We have already discussed the ethical concern of lawyer–client confidentiality in Chapter 1. This chapter covers five more ethics issues around legal AI:

1. Duty of Competency
2. Duty of Communication
3. Duty to Supervise / Unauthorized Practice of Law
4. Duty of Loyalty
5. The Issue of Bias

These are big topics, and each invites analysis 10 times as long as we present here. As leading legal ethics expert Professor Stephen Gillers says, "It is like going to a banquet with a menu of a dozen tasty dishes but getting only a forkful of each one." We hope your forkfuls will inspire you to learn more on these important issues.

Duty of Competency

Lawyers have an obligation to "zealously . . . protect and pursue a client's legitimate interests."[1] To do this, they need to be competent at their jobs. Obviously, this means they need to know (or know how to find) relevant law. A number of jurisdictions also require that lawyers be competent with relevant technology. Given the increased adoption of artificial intelligence in areas of law practice, it's becoming a must-know area for lawyers. For example, in the United States, American Bar Association Model Rule 1.1 states that "competent representation requires the legal knowledge, skill, thoroughness and preparation reasonably necessary for the representation." In 2012, the ABA added a comment to this Rule, stating that "to maintain the requisite knowledge and skill, lawyers should keep abreast of changes in the law and its practice, including the benefits and risks associated with relevant technology." To date, 37 states have adopted this comment, meaning lawyers in those states need to be appropriately competent around relevant technology to be "competent" lawyers. In 2019, The Federation of Law Societies of Canada adopted similar model language.[2]

This duty makes sense. Imagine a US corporate lawyer not bothering to track developments in Delaware case law around director's duties. They would clearly not be competently doing their job if they had to advise the board of a Delaware corporation, even if they were very knowledgeable about other areas of law. They would also not be doing the job competently if they were fully up on the law only as of three years ago, or if they were simply too busy to read new cases. If a new, relevant case comes out of the Delaware Court of Chancery or the Supreme Court, they need to read up on it, period. Using appropriate technology (often including AI) is central to doing a decent job at litigation discovery, due diligence, and legal research (among other areas). You increasingly can't do them "right" without the appropriate technology, in the same way that you can't properly advise if you don't know the law. Lawyers are not allowed to not do their job or do a poor job because they've always done something a certain way.

Duty of Communication

ABA Model Rule 1.4 addresses communication with clients. It requires lawyers "reasonably consult with the client about the means by which the client's objectives are to be accomplished." Some have asserted that this obligation means that lawyers need to tell clients when they are using AI.

> *A lawyer should obtain approval from the client before using AI, and this consent must be informed. The discussion should include the risks and limitations of the AI tool. In certain circumstances, a lawyer's decision not to use AI also may need to be communicated to the client if using AI would benefit the client. Indeed, the lawyer's failure to use AI could implicate ABA Model Rule 1.5, which requires lawyer's fees to be reasonable. Failing to use AI technology that materially reduces the costs of providing legal services arguably could result in a lawyer charging an unreasonable fee to a client.[3]*

While we don't disagree with the "reasonable fee" point, we are skeptical about lawyers always needing to tell clients that they are using AI in their representation. Should lawyers feel obligated to tell clients whether they use Lexis, Westlaw, Fastcase, or Casetext for their legal research? What about if they switched from Westlaw Classic to AI-enabled Westlaw Edge? Would that trigger a client communication requirement? Or is this just business as usual? The rule requiring client communications is subject to a reasonableness standard. There will be situations where lawyers should inform their clients about using AI, and others where it's unnecessary. When lawyers are doing work the same way they traditionally would have done it in the past, but simply supplemented by AI, we're skeptical they need to inform. For example, if lawyers are reviewing contracts page-by-page within a contract analysis software system (which our research finds still yields more accurate review in 20–30% less time), they are basically doing what a client expects, just better. On the other hand, if they are using AI as the only set of "eyes" on a particular group of agreements (e.g., a folder of nondisclosure agreements or customer contracts they otherwise wouldn't review), it makes sense for them to be very forthright with their clients about their approach, and the risks and benefits of relying on AI.

In our experience, we have found that clients *like* hearing about their lawyers using AI and other efficiency tools. So, instead of thinking about whether or not you *have* to tell your clients you are using AI, you should consider telling them because it will make them happy. Ralph Pais, Technology Transactions partner at Fenwick & West (and a Kira user since 2016) says, "I have often found clients care that we use AI. In fact, when I told executives at a client we were going to use Kira on a deal and explained what it was, the GC said, 'I haven't met 'her' yet, but I am glad we have her on our team.'" Jonathan Klein, chair of the Mergers and Acquisitions Group at DLA Piper (and also a Kira user since 2016), concurs:

> We have found that clients are very receptive to hearing that their lawyers use AI and other tools that increase efficiency. In fact, increasingly, clients expect their law firms to utilize AI and other technology to promote efficient and cost effective outcomes. With that in mind, we regularly promote our use of AI technology as an important and regular part of our client offerings.

Duty to Supervise / Unauthorized Practice of Law

In most jurisdictions, only lawyers are allowed to do legal work. Some captivating unauthorized practice of law (UPL) stories involve people pretending to be lawyers. More interesting—to us, at least—is how rules restricting legal work to human lawyers interact with innovations like DIY law tools and AI-based artificial lawyers. We're willing to bet we'll see cases on whether AI can commit the unauthorized practice of law, but haven't yet. So let's look at parallel situations, specifically providers of DIY legal content like Nolo and LegalZoom, as well as human eDiscovery reviewers. Are they providing legal advice, and can they be restricted from doing so?

In 1998, the Supreme Court of Texas' Unauthorized Practice of Law subcommittee ordered Nolo Press, publishers of legal self-help books, to explain why the sale of its books and software should not be prohibited. This committee claimed that Nolo's products put individuals at risk because consumers saw Nolo as a legitimate legal resource.

In June of 1999 the Texas Legislature passed HB1507, a bill exempting self-help materials from UPL prosecution, providing the material contains disclaimers that the material does not constitute actual legal advice. Nolo's products had carried such disclaimers for many years. The case against Nolo was officially dropped on September 21, 1999.[4]

LegalZoom has also had to deal with a number of UPL legal claims and complaints over the past decade, including in California, North Carolina, Arkansas, and Missouri. LegalZoom, which is essentially an expert system, continues to provide self-help forms in all of the United States and in the United Kingdom. They also provide access to licensed attorneys for a fee. The LegalZoom website includes a disclaimer (as of the writing of this book) reading: "We are not a law firm or a substitute for an attorney or law firm. We cannot provide any kind of advice, explanation, opinion, or recommendation about possible legal rights, remedies, defenses, options, selection of forms or strategies."[5]

Unauthorized practice of law cases against technology providers aren't restricted to the United States. In late 2019, a regional court in Cologne, Germany, sided with the Hanseatic Bar Association against Smartlaw.de. As Richard Tromans of ArtificialLawyer.com describes, "The Bar claims that tech-based platforms like this cannot provide sufficient legal certainty for a client as they rely on an automated Q&A expert system to fill in a contract or other legal document template. In short, unless you have lawyers involved in contract creation then it should not be allowed, they say."[6] Tromans continues:

> In relation to the case in Hamburg, on winning their case against Smartlaw, the Bar published a press release (in German) claiming that what the company did was 'an inadmissible legal service and therefore a violation of the Legal Services Act (RDG).'
> It went on to say that a core reason for their case was 'the protection of the legal profession from unqualified competitors'.
> Perhaps most importantly for legal tech companies is this part of their statement, which in effect says that digital contract systems are incapable of offering a reliable legal document on their own.

'When drafting legally secure . . . contracts, it is usually necessary to clarify the relevant facts in cooperation with the client. . . . This cannot be provided by a computer that asks different questions about the desired contract design in a question and answer system and then delivers a contract that has been compiled considering the answers,' they said.

This ruling is under appeal as of the writing of this book.[7] The Bar also pointed out that there was a pricing aspect, with the tech platform offering services at a very low cost compared to regular lawyers.

Unauthorized practice of law cases aren't the only ones relevant to how a court will someday decide whether a legal AI is doing impermissible legal work. In *Lola v. Skadden, Arps, Slate, Meagher & Flom LLP* (2015), the Second Circuit considered whether a lawyer doing technology assisted litigation document review was engaged in the practice of law. David Lola, a document reviewer, asserted that he was not doing legal work, and so should be entitled to overtime pay. Here, one of the most influential courts in the United States held:

A fair reading of the complaint in the light most favorable to Lola is that he provided services that a machine could have provided. The parties themselves agreed at oral argument that an individual who, in the course of reviewing discovery documents, undertakes tasks that could otherwise be performed entirely by a machine cannot be said to engage in the practice of law.

This ruling is probably the most important indication of how courts will view whether a machine can commit UPL, at least in the USA. If a machine cannot, by definition, engage in the practice of law, how can software ever be responsible for unauthorized practice, even when consumers use it without mediation or oversight by a lawyer?

Today, most legal AI with significant adoption tends to be tools used with lawyers somewhere in the loop (apart from the expert systems powering offerings like LegalZoom or Smartlaw.de). For example, in eDiscovery, many (but not all) contract analysis use cases and judicial prediction systems all have a human in the loop. There is no prohibition on non-lawyers (like a legal secretary or paralegal) doing legal work, as long as a lawyer supervises them. This should be the same with an AI—entirely unproblematic if used to do legal work under supervision of a lawyer. Over time, we expect to see more and more direct-to-(non-lawyer)-consumer legal AIs, and it will be fascinating to see how these are regulated, if at all. Lawyers often get to regulate themselves. They are supposed to do so for the benefit of the public, but there can be real tension here between the needs of lawyers (who tend to be helped by less competition) and what's good for society at large. Direct-to-consumer legal AI raises serious questions, including whether the AI has the requisite legal knowledge; whether it should have the obligations that come from being a lawyer, such as the adherence to the high principles and rules; whether AI should be regulated; and whether the people who build or train legal AI should have to be lawyers.

As the legal system works through these questions, it may face governments weighing in, as happened in Texas after its attack on Nolo, or occurred in the United Kingdom, where legislatures dramatically liberalized rules around who can do legal services in 2007.

Duty of Loyalty

A core lawyer duty is loyalty to clients. ABA Model Rule 1.7 states (in part):

> *Loyalty and independent judgment are essential elements in the lawyer's relationship to a client. Concurrent conflicts of interest can arise from the lawyer's responsibilities to another client, a former client or a third person or from the lawyer's own interests.*

This duty is so central that it can even be an ethical breach for a lawyer to help their spouse in a suit against a client of their firm, even when they themselves have never worked for the client.[8]

Should AI be subject to these same restrictions? If AI is trained in the course of working for one client's project, can it be used against that same client in another situation? This is not as far-fetched as it initially sounds. If, for example, your firm has a bank client, and you've trained AI while working on their projects, and you sometimes represent other clients borrowing money from that bank, you could end up in this situation. *Is it okay that the firm benefits from training an AI in the course of client work?* Can you use AI that has been trained while working for clients when you're working against them (presumably under a conflict waiver)?

If using the AI helps the client (by, for example, getting them higher-quality or faster and better value work), it seems unproblematic if the firm also benefits from its AI models getting more training. Non-fee benefits regularly accrue to lawyers when they work without AI. They improve their skills, build precedent documents that they draw from for other projects, and burnish their reputations. It also seems unproblematic that AI is used on both sides, as long as no client confidential information is exposed in the course of using the AI in an adverse situation. (The ethical considerations of client confidentiality are discussed further in Chapter 1.) The AI learning here is no different than that which a lawyer learns from each of their projects. In this case the AI is learning nothing more than an associate who works on multiple projects. In fact, it may be even less problematic with AI, because the AI is not going to remember specifically "dangerous stuff" that a human might. It will also remember the material from the training exactly the same way every time without any added bias.

Let's now consider a trickier situation (as described in Chapter 5 on amplifying expertise). We anticipate lawyers will increasingly train and share their knowledge in the form of AI models, enabling them to work on matters without having to actually "work" on them. Imagine a firm trains their AI in the course of doing client work (the AI makes the firm's lawyers faster and more accurate at this work; it benefits their clients). The firm realizes it has built a quality AI model that could be useful to others, so they make it available for purchase on an AI marketplace, for, say, $0.25 per judgment made, payable on a pay-per-use basis. Some of the firm's clients "buy" and use the model. Great—the firm is making extra money, without having to do additional work, and strengthening their brand with users of the model along the way. Another firm "buys" the model. Great again—same advantages. The other firm uses the model in a manner adverse to one of the clients whose work the selling firm trained it on. Problem?

The lawyer's duty of loyalty stems from the systematic design of the legal system, where different participants have different roles—some as zealous advocates, some as neutral arbiters. Conflicts have the potential to throw this system off-balance. Even the appearance of a potential conflict undermines the system's credibility. The majority of artificial intelligence systems, however, have no feelings or a concept of loyalty. AI doesn't care who it is working for—it will work the same irrespective. Accordingly, we should not care whether it works in adverse situations (where we would not allow human lawyers to act), since it will not behave differently because of its feelings or divided loyalties, where a human lawyer might.

Overall, situations like these, where the duty of loyalty interacts with lawyers training AI, seem ripe for lots of further analysis in law review articles.

Whose Mistake Is This Anyway?

AI systems make mistakes. Who should be responsible when they do?

This is a function of contract, tort, and product liability law more than anything else. Typically, AI systems' user agreements limit their vendor's warranties and liability. There are good reasons for this. First, most responsible vendors know their system makes errors and wouldn't pledge otherwise. Second, AI systems often supplement lawyers and are not really making the final decisions that would lead to liability.[9] Third, vendors would have to charge a lot more to take on the risk (though they could potentially cover themselves by purchasing their own "errors and omissions" insurance policies).

The Issue of Bias

Key decisions made with the use of AI can have a significant impact on many people. Therefore, any bias in the system can raise serious issues. There is a lot of confusion over how to solve such problems.

Reporting on the topic has ranged from blaming algorithms, to blaming computer scientists, to blaming companies using and selling AI. So where is the problem? It's certainly possible to explicitly write an algorithm that is biased against a group of people. For example, rule-based systems in which humans craft the rules can have hard coded biases that are intentionally included. These scenarios, however, are uncommon; we believe few people intentionally try to create biased algorithms and systems. More importantly, most modern AI *learns on its own*. Humans rarely build these systems by hand. Instead, a generic mathematical framework is applied to data in order to produce an AI system.

The mathematical framework itself is not the source of the bias, nor is it "built in" to any algorithm by hand. Rather, bias comes into play when you *apply AI techniques to data*. Here, the bias is actually coming from the *data* the system is learning from. Another way to put this is that the bias *always comes from people*, whether from data generated by people, or in—rule-based systems—potentially by the person writing the rules.

Since the majority of modern AI is based on machine learning (where AI is built by learning from data), let's focus the rest of the discussion on these systems. In this scenario, the source of the bias tends more often to be the *data than the nature of the specific algorithm being used (though the latter can matter and can be hard to get transparent information on)*. The responsibility for addressing it is with the people who are applying machine learning algorithms to that data. Consider a real example. In the United States, there is a need to predict the likelihood for re-offense when deciding whether to grant a person parole. COMPASS, a popular tool for this task, was found to be biased against Black defendants. Even if all other factors were equal, simply changing the color of a defendant's skin would cause the system to predict a higher re-offense rate. A criticism of tools like COMPASS is that they are black boxes, where the vendor doesn't always explain the techniques they use. However, we know many tools like COMPASS use machine learning to predict re-offense rates. These tools are trained on historical data about people granted parole. The bias in this case was already built into this historical data. In many cases, existing systematic bias in the prison system, or other societal issues, results in the data having this outcome. That is, however, a correlation, not a causation. It's when the system making predictions treats it as causation that the problem arises. One upside is that by attempting to automate re-offense predictions, the existing bias problems were brought to light.

Solutions to AI Bias

Given all of this, is it possible to remove bias from machine learning systems? Although this is an area of ongoing research, there are already several techniques available today that can help remove bias. The first step is to *test for bias*. In the case of recidivism rate, you can test by changing the skin color or gender of a particular individual and then look at whether the prediction changes. Doing that on a large enough number of individuals will tell you if the model is biased. Detection is always the first step. This makes sense: testing is a critical part of building machine learning systems.

One of the simplest solutions is to remove input traits that you don't want the system to use to determine an outcome. In many systems, these traits are called *features* and represent properties of the world from which you are trying to learn. For example, if you're trying to make a prediction about whether someone being released from jail will become a re-offender, you might use features such as the person's gender, skin color, education level, age, and so forth. In the previous example, the system learned to correlate skin color with recidivism rate. As humans, we know that this is not a causal relationship, and it is an undesirable outcome. To fix this, we can simply remove skin color from the set of features we supply to the algorithm and thus force it not to consider that in its predictive model. This is a useful technique, but isn't the end of the story. It's still possible for machine learning systems to find secondary unwanted correlations. For instance, perhaps people of a given skin color tend to live in the same zip code, and you use zip code as an input. Even though you've removed skin color as input, the system can still learn that people in a given zip code have a higher recidivism rate. The connection to skin color is less obvious, but it might still be a problem. This is why bias is a hard problem. That said, this technique does help to significantly reduce bias in machine learning systems.

Another common technique is to modify the training data. For example, with recidivism rates, you could make sure that people of all skin colors are equally represented. There isn't always enough training data to erase bias, but in many cases it can help. It is often good practice for attaining a highly accurate machine learning system anyway.

Norm Judah, a former chief technology officer at Microsoft, has a simple, but excellent idea: make sure your data science team is diverse. A diverse team will be more likely to think about and find these bias issues. (Also, it has been shown that diverse teams often generate better solutions.)

Ethics Review: An Ongoing Issue

Ethics in law has been, and will continue to be, a conversation starter, especially when it pertains to machine learning and AI. Even in what appears to be the most obvious scenario, where something seems clearly right or wrong, you are likely to find someone questioning it or presenting a conflicting viewpoint. Much remains open to interpretation.

The subjects of ethics and bias come up often with technology. What is permissible legally and what is permissible ethically often fall into different categories. The glut of new technology has resulted in numerous questions of ethical behavior brought about by the use of emails and even cell phones where, for example, there is a question of who has the right to read your emails or your texts, or who owns the rights to a photograph or video. It is our belief, through our own experiences working with AI for more than a decade, that the question of ethical behavior stems from the actions and attitudes of people, not machines. For that reason, it's imperative that lawyers work strictly with their client's best interests in mind and recognize that AI and other tools of technology are just that, tools. They are invaluable assistants, and they are here to stay, but they still don't make the rules, or completely train themselves—that's still the responsibility of humans.

LEGAL AI FOR SOCIAL GOOD

By Noah Waisberg and John Lute

Legal AI is having a positive impact on lawyers, making them more productive, better able to serve their clients, and more prosperous. Can legal AI also positively influence society? There are many examples from the Legal AI community where AI is doing just that; encouraging gender diversity, helping with issues such as elder abuse, and bringing transparency.

Docket Alarm, an AI-powered Legal Research solution (owned by Fastcase), realized early on that it could easily analyze the gender diversity of entire legal practice areas from the public record. In its database of over 400 million litigation proceedings and intellectual property prosecution records, Docket Alarm has a list of the attorneys of record for each proceeding. Using AI to analyze attorney first names, the company was able to estimate the gender breakdown.

In 2017, through a relationship with the PTAB Bar Association (a patent litigation–related bar association), Docket Alarm published results suggesting that only 22% of partners at major US law firms were women, and 55 of the top 100 law firms had less than 10% of their attorney court appearances made by women.

The PTAB Bar Association published a report (citing Docket Alarm's research), which was then publicized by a number of law firms and publications.

As the report gained further traction, Docket Alarm received calls from a diverse set of organizations, and is now assisting nonprofits, academics, and law firm pro-bono departments on their own public service data analysis projects, helping them uncover insights to be used as evidence when advocating for a better legal system.

Another example of legal AI being put to a positive societal use is the Legal Risk Detector. It is a web-based legal health "check-up" tool that helps service providers screen seniors for potential legal issues, such as financial exploitation, consumer, housing, and health care matters. It's designed to more comprehensively serve an elder population that is vulnerable to various forms of abuse, but difficult to serve through traditional legal services. The tool was initially developed from a Georgetown Law student assignment, and then further enhanced by a coalition of organizations, including Neota Logic, whose expert system technology powers the tool. After receiving grant funding from the Department of Justice, the Legal Risk Detector is now in use in five US states and has inspired several similar elder law applications around the country.

Kira Systems has worked with the Campaign Zero organization, a group that aims to provide people with the information and tools they need to end police violence. In June 2020, Campaign Zero used Kira to review over 600 police union contracts and Law Enforcement Officers' Bills of Rights (LEOBRs) from 20 US states and found six common problems that raise accountability issues including: short expiration dates on complaints, limited oversight and discipline of officers, erased misconduct records, police misconduct cases paid for with public funds, preferential access to evidence for implicated officers, and unfair interrogation procedures. Campaign Zero were able to review these contracts with 70% greater efficiency than they would have manually, as well as create a smart database that embedded the data in their website. The speed at which they were able to review these contracts and surface the data was important in their effort to enable journalists, activists, policy makers, academics, and others to take action in the moment that police reform was a national story and concern.

Sometimes it's easy to lose sight of the greater opportunity legal AI provides. These examples are a reminder that the role and opportunity of legal AI is not just to help lawyers in their day-to-day jobs but to benefit all society.

Notes

1. ABA. 2000. Preamble: A lawyer's responsibilities, para 9, *Model Rules of Professional Conduct: Preamble & Scope*. American Bar Association. https://www.americanbar .org/groups/professional_responsibility/publications/model_rules_of_profes- sional_conduct/model_rules_of_professional_conduct_preamble_scope/
2. Robert Ambrogi tends to periodically update his LawSites blog (https://www .lawsitesblog.com) with jurisdictions that require lawyers be competent with rel- evant technology.

3. Cerny, J., S. Delchin, and H. Nguyen. 2019. Legal ethics in the use of artificial intelligence. SquirePattonBoggs.com (February). https://www.squirepattonboggs.com/-/media/files/insights/publications/2019/02/legal-ethics-in-the-use-of-artificial-intelligence/legalethics_feb2019.pdf

4. Blog.Nolo.com. 2011. The Brief story of *Texas vs. Nolo*. Nolo (April 11). https://blog.nolo.com/blog/2011/04/11/the-brief-story-of-texas-vs-nolo/

5. Shipman, C. 2019. Unauthorized practice of law claims against LegalZoom—Who do these lawsuits protect, and is the rule outdated? *Georgetown Legal Ethics Journal* (November 24). https://www.law.georgetown.edu/legal-ethics-journal/wp-content/uploads/sites/24/2019/11/GT-GJLE190045.pdf

6. LegalTech on Trial—Regional German bar wins ban on contract platforms. 2019. Artificial Lawyer (October 10). https://www.artificiallawyer.com/2019/10/10/legaltech-on-trial-regional-german-bar-wins-ban-on-contract-platforms

7. Doc Generation Ban – German Court Seems Favourable to Wolters Kluwer on UPL Claim. 2020. Artificial Lawyer (May 18). https://www.artificiallawyer.com/2020/05/18/doc-generation-ban-german-court-seems-favourable-to-wolters-kluwer-on-upl-claim/

8. FlatWorld Interactives LLC v. Apple Inc., Case No. 12-cv-01956-WHO (N.D. Cal. Aug. 7, 2013).

9. On this point, Professor Richard Moorhead notes that this raises an issue of mutually assured irresponsibility. The human relies on the machine unthinkingly, and the machine and its designers rely on the unlikely protection of human supervision.

PART II

The Proof

AI technologies are delivering
results today

CHAPTER 7

eDiscovery

What It Is and How AI Is Continuing to Transform How It Works for You

By Dera Nevin*

In the imagination, a trial is a gripping contest between a lawyer and a witness, as illustrated in movies like *A Few Good Men*. In the Anglo-American legal system, trials are used to pit rival positions against each other, with each side testing the other's story and a judge or jury deciding where the truth lies. Before trial, the process of taking deposition serves the same purpose. For example, in *The Social Network,* we see an illustration of the deposition process and how this is used to have each side lay out its case orally, through testimony.

Television and films are visual media, and so it's not surprising that these present the visual dimensions of finding and presenting the facts of a case. However, lawyers have at their disposal three forms of evidence. The first is *testimonial* evidence, which is what we typically see on TV. This kind of evidence involves a witness telling their story or version of events, and a lawyer cross-examining that witness to poke holes in the story, to test it for reliability. A second form of evidence is *demonstrative*, which consists of actual evidence (such as a bloody glove from a murder trial) or an illustration of evidence (such as a blueprint of a building, or an illustration of a how a machine works). Demonstrative evidence is things brought into a courtroom, or places that a jury is taken to get a better sense of what might have happened.

A form of demonstrative evidence that stands on its own is the third kind of evidence and that's *documentary* evidence, which can be understood as testimony in written form. Contracts, letters, purchase orders, or anything

*Dera Nevin has served as eDiscovery Counsel and Director of Information Governance at an Am Law 50 firm in New York City, and has practiced eDiscovery internationally. This chapter is drawn from materials delivered at several speeches, including before bar associations in New York and Canada. Comments here reflect her personal views.

reduced to writing might be documentary evidence. It's easy to underestimate the importance of documentary evidence, because it is often introduced through witnesses, such as when a document is in front of a witness and the witness is asked, "Do you recognize this document?" However, documents do a significant amount of work in introducing evidence into a deposition or trial; often, much of the testimony of witnesses involves getting them to identify and accept the content of documents as a mechanism for proving both the document itself and establishing the truth of its contents. This is a way that the documents are "proved" and a trier of fact—a judge or jury—can rely on the content of the documents in deciding the case.

As more information is created and comes into existence using computerized means, eDiscovery is used to find, understand, and present this electronically created information during the course of a lawsuit. The prevalence of electronic information has given rise to a number of challenges within each of the discovery and the trial processes. For example:

- How does a lawyer find and review the potential evidence?
- How is this electronic information put into evidence in depositions and at trial?
- It's very easy to delete electronic information, so how do we know the other side isn't hiding or suppressing evidence?
- Sometimes, computers just "break," or become obsolete over the course of a lawsuit—how do we keep that evidence intact?

eDiscovery has had to solve for all these problems, as well as being the bridge between the need to put information that has been created on a computer into a court proceeding.

eDiscovery moved into the mainstream when more and more people started using email in ordinary business and personal dealings, and then brought claims to court that required that information to become evidence. When the documentary evidence that lawyers would otherwise need to build and present their cases started to be located in email, lawyers had to figure out how to find emails. Since most emails are not filed in filing cabinets, the questions were:

- How do we find and present emails in the courtroom?
- How do we get that evidence in front of triers of facts?
- How do I find what I need and keep track of it?

This last question has been particularly important as the amount of email has exploded. Today, eDiscovery has become even more complicated because there are so many places to create electronic information. Everything from Facebook to Twitter to YouTube to Slack to TikTok could include information that could be used to help either a jury or a judge decide a case. Today, even criminal trials may involve voice recordings captured on a personal assistant such as Alexa or Google Home, and we've all read about cases where the police or FBI has wanted to access a suspect's iPhone or other computerized device. In such cases, the police or FBI are wanting those devices to perform investigative or eDiscovery actions, in order to locate potential evidence that could eventually make its way into a courtroom as documentary evidence.

eDiscovery helps you find answers to the basic questions:

- How do I find the information?
- Where is it in the computer or computer system?
- How do I search through the information once I've found it?
- How do I get it into a format where I can use it for dispute resolution such as in a courtroom?

My eDiscovery Roots

I was a junior lawyer in the late 1990s when the legal industry was just starting to grapple with the fact that, increasingly, clients were using computers and this would impact locating evidence for use in trial, and on questions of how to find, manage and present evidence that had been created using computers. In larger firms, while the senior lawyers are the ones who will stand in court and present the case, it was (and still is) the job of the junior lawyers and paraprofessionals (such as paralegals and technicians) to do the work behind the scenes and create the materials that these senior lawyers will use. As a practical matter, that means junior lawyers read all the documents—or emails—to find the ones that are useful to put into the record during a deposition or at trial. Once upon a time, junior lawyers would go to record centers, open filing cabinets and flip through papers. However, as more and more information started to be created using computers, increasingly the task of these junior lawyers became to somehow accomplish the same thing but against emails, electronic accounting systems, and other computer-created information, such as documents made using Microsoft Word. I was among the young lawyers that had to figure out how to obtain, work with, and present electronic evidence; this was an emerging field that became known as *eDiscovery* for "electronic discovery"—discovery of electronic information. *Discovery* is the process of finding evidence for trial, and "eDiscovery" became the process of finding *electronic* evidence for trial.

Of course, as a junior lawyer, if you get experience doing something that others don't know how to do, you can make an opportunity to do much more of it, because you might become the first person people think about when they see the same problem. If you do something as a junior lawyer, you start to do it again and again, and thus can develop an expertise in it. I can't remember a time in my legal career when I wasn't doing eDiscovery. Since any computer-based device could create and hold potentially important electronic evidence, I started to see new opportunities everywhere. I could see that portable devices that people carried might hold important non-email evidence, and I was part of a team to first put Blackberry PIN-to-PIN messages in evidence. I was among the first to put Facebook and Twitter posts into evidence. I was also among the first to put automotive black box data into evidence. The reason I was able to do this was because I always recognized what could hold a potential source of evidence, and I've never been afraid to go to a computer-based system to find evidence. Having this skill gave me the opportunity to be on the front lines and to try some interesting issues in cases.

Because, as a lawyer, it is important to make sure that any electronic document met the legal criteria required for "proof," I paid a lot of attention to how new technology worked. I knew that eventually I'd see that technology in a litigation context and I'd need to do eDiscovery against it. I've worked with technology companies to design and improve eDiscovery systems, to make them more reliable in how they handle and manage evidence, and also how user-friendly and responsive these are to lawyers' needs. I also have had the opportunity to serve as a neutral expert in a case to help the trier of fact understand the validity of computer-based evidence that's put into the courtroom, and whether the court can rely on it. Over the many years I worked directly in eDiscovery, I shifted from trying cases myself, to instead working for several law firms running eDiscovery departments and operations, including the technology used to handle computer-based evidence and providing legal services about data and electronic information more generally.

How AI Turned Traditional Discovery on Its Head

Discovery has been an essential part of the American legal process for a long time—it's putting all the pieces of the case together from visiting locations and interviewing witnesses and taking their testimony, to asking for documentary discovery. Recently, the process has changed from doing a lot of physical leg work to working electronically at the computer, because computers are a major feature of modern life. They have changed our modes of communication, and even how we do transactions. For instance, many of us do our banking, investing, and shopping electronically. That means, for any dispute involving those activities that go to trial, the evidence will exist electronically. A lot of people will say "electronic discovery is discovery," but when it comes to using such discovery in a court of law, different techniques are required when you're dealing with electronic evidence rather than documents printed to paper.

eDiscovery really consists of several distinct but related steps, and these have been cataloged in something called the Electronic Discovery Reference Model (or EDRM). The first step is identification. You first have to figure out where your electronic evidence is and what sources it is in. It may be somewhere in your email box, but where? Perhaps it has been moved to a file folder somewhere in your hard drive. Could it be saved on your phone? Is it in the cloud? Is there possible data on Facebook? In a Box account? On a dated computer using software that is 10 years old? Much of this step actually involves asking a lot of questions and recording the answers, but to ask the right questions, you need to know something about the technology and how people might use it. For example, you might not discover that key messages between people were communicated using WhatsApp if you don't know what WhatsApp is or how it works.

The next steps are preservation and collection. These activities can be quite technical and often lawyers and technologists will partner together to ensure the evidence isn't deleted and is gathered up using methods that preserve the evidence and its integrity. I sometimes call this the "preserving the crime scene" part of the process and this analogy works—it can be understood as the digital equivalent of putting up yellow police tape and systematically taking the evidence from one place and moving it to another.

The next step involves search and review and lawyers get involved here in a big way. AI systems can play a major role in these steps. Once you collect all the emails, Word documents, and social media posts, you generally dump these into a specialized application and run all kinds of searches across these data to find what might be helpful to understand and build the case. The information retrieval process is very important because you need to find the precise messages or the specific evidence that you are looking for, so that you have the documents that will be put into evidence.

AI can help here to manage what can be an enormous volume of electronic data, and can also be used to make the search more precise in situations where you might not know what you are looking for. Typically, people search by keyword, but there can be two problems in eDiscovery. Where keywords are generic and data volumes large, such as millions and millions of emails, a keyword can still leave a lot of email to read. As recently as 10 years ago, you'd see 200 junior lawyers reading through hundreds of thousands or millions of messages to find the 75 messages that might be responsive and need to be put into evidence. It was tedious, time-consuming, and not always fruitful.

But a bigger problem is that the lawyers might not know what keywords to enter, for two reasons. First, it's hard to come up with a complete list of all the possible words that might help you find what you are searching for. This is what I call the "dog problem." If you were looking for emails about dogs, you could put in the keyword "dog," but you would risk missing things if the people corresponding in that email didn't use the specific word "dog" in a given message. For example, there might be an email about a dog but if it says, "I'm supposed to take Rover for a walk but I can't find the leash," the keyword "dog" won't retrieve that message. Second, you just might not know what keywords to enter. For example, if you have suspicion of fraud, but you don't know how the fraud operated, or who was involved, what keywords would you use to find this evidence? You could use a whole bunch of synonyms to try to find it, but this could be very unreliable. (It's rare that people write out emails saying, "Here is how I am going to commit the fraud"). For example, in the Enron dataset, which consists of a public set of data released during and after the criminal trials associated with the collapse of that company, many of the special purpose vehicles (SPVs) that were being used in the scheme had pet names such as Raptor and Football. In a fraud case, it's unlikely you'd think to enter a keyword relating to a popular sport.

This search and review phase is where computerized techniques involving AI have had the most impact on eDiscovery, and where AI is experiencing increasing adoption rates every year. AI helps with several aspects of the information retrieval and review step. What exists now are (i) computers with highly specialized search software and (ii) review software, both of which incorporate AI to categorize and classify large volumes of information accurately. And AI can be used to augment and improve search capability.

The prevalence of this advanced technology for use in electronic discovery means there is no longer a need for armies of junior lawyers to mine for data by reviewing each email separately. These AI systems can be run by a smaller number of lawyers who are trained to use that software.

The final steps of the eDiscovery process is production and presentation. Once the large volume of electronic information has been searched and reviewed to find what is necessary, it needs to be given to the other side, or prepared to be presented during a deposition or trial. Potential and actual evidence is labeled and sorted so that it can be retrieved quickly during the pressure of a trial, or so that all the parties can find it quickly. Each document, page, or element is labeled so that people can understand which party produced it and whether or not it's been accepted as evidence or still needs to be proved.

The Role of AI in eDiscovery Search and Review

Let's spend a bit more time describing modern electronic evidence systems, how they work, and the role that AI plays in them. Let's suppose, for example, there's a case that involves allegations that a particular model of car has a defective braking system and that there are millions of such cars on the road that need to be recalled. In such a dispute, customers might want costs of repairs or, if there were injuries, people might be claiming compensation or damages. Even though millions of cars may be affected, this claim might be consolidated into one class action case. Let's think about the evidence that might need to be handled to bring that to a hearing. First, you'd have records of all the cars that were made and sold and you'd need some way to tie those cars to purchasers or owners, to know who was a proper party to the lawsuit and/or who might be compensated. There also would be evidence of the car's design, including all the braking systems; this might involve engineering diagrams and all the records of the design and testing of the airbags. It's possible emails from the engineers, quality control, and production personnel would need to be collected, reviewed, and produced. The plaintiff's lawyers might allege that someone in the company knew the airbag was defective. If so, emails from customer support and others alleged to have handled that inquiry could be implicated. Even in this thought experiment, you can start to see that possibly tens to hundreds of personnel might have relevant emails, possibly generated over a time period of years (from the point at which the brakes were first designed to the time of the claim), and there could be many other kinds of electronic records involved as well. In fact, in a case such as this, tens of millions of emails could be collected and would need to be reviewed. To review all of these could take years; and really, most of the emails would not be relevant to the issues in the litigation. Generally, entire email boxes are collected (i.e., they take all of a person's emails), rather than only the "key" messages, because it's not always clear at collection what the "key" messages are.

AI review systems could help in such a case as follows: using only a small subset of email records, such as those located from keywords, a lawyer will review and label (or tag) as relevant those messages that relate to the dispute about the allegedly faulty brakes. The computer then "scans" the words in the message and properties of the message such as who sent and received it to "learn" the criteria that the lawyers think is important or "relevant." With such AI systems, the more lawyers "train" the AI, the more criteria the computer uses to "learn" to understand "relevance." Once the AI is trained, the AI will scan the entire corpus of records that have not been reviewed by a lawyer to retrieve those that seem to be similar to the criteria in the emails that the lawyer tagged as relevant; the lawyer can then review only that subset rather than the millions and millions that were collected. This can save a lot of time and also a lot of money. If there is any doubt that the computer/AI has not pulled all the potentially relevant messages forward based on its training, the lawyers can look at what was "left behind" and sample this by reviewing a subset of those messages. If most of them are irrelevant, this can give the lawyer confidence that the system worked and that not every message needs to be reviewed. I've made it seem simple here, but these systems contain records of their own efficacy and proof; they will generate reports on the math and statistical models they use, which can be introduced into evidence so that parties can review how the computers were trained to categorize messages.

Although these systems are becoming more widely adopted, it has taken the legal community almost a decade to accept them. Now there are judicial opinions which indicate that courts accept this process, too.

TECHNOLOGY ASSISTED REVIEW (TAR)

By Noah Waisberg and Dr. Alexander Hudek

Technology assisted review (TAR) has made a significant impact on the legal field for nearly a decade, particularly when it comes to document review and data analysis. TAR is proving to save attorneys, and their clients, significant time and expense as it pertains to the process of data retrieval. As mentioned, it has taken some time for TAR to be accepted in law. Let's look at the influential events that helped it get there.

A Groundbreaking Article

Maura Grossman and Gordon Cormack wrote an article in *The Richmond Journal of Law and Technology* titled "Technology Assisted Review in eDiscovery Can Be More Effective and More Efficient Than Exhaustive Manual Review."[1] The article presented evidence that technology assisted processes yield results superior to those of exhaustive manual review, as measured by recall and precision as well as the *F-score,* a summary measure combining recall and precision.

It concluded that "technology-assisted review can (and does) yield more accurate results than exhaustive manual review, with much lower effort." In particular, the superior processes in the study used a combination of computer and human input.

Despite the evidence within the article, and some technology companies developing and positioning tools under the banner of TAR, no court at that time had yet approved the use of TAR in the courtroom. In addition, no lawyers had stepped up and stated that they wanted to use this in court, as they were concerned with the risk of being challenged in the courtroom and even within their own firms.

The DaSilva Moore Case

Another key contributor to TAR's rise in acceptance was a 2012 legal case in the United States District Court for the Southern District of New York. The now well-known case *Moore v. Publicis Groupe*[2] explicitly recognized the use of predictive coding technology (i.e., computer-assisted review) as an appropriate method to satisfy a producing party's review obligations. Magistrate Judge Andrew Peck held that computer-assisted review could now be considered judicially approved for use in appropriate cases. The review method was upheld, not because it included predictive coding technology but because the technology was applied in an appropriate manner likely to produce reliable results at a proportional cost. TAR had validation.

eDiscovery in Action

I first began recognizing what could be done with this kind of AI technology when the technology was first introduced to the market over 10 years ago. The use of that technology allowed me to automate a step that I used to have to do manually, and saved me weeks of time and effort, allowing me to get information to a client faster, cheaper, and more accurately.

I was helping a client with what I believed to be an insider trading or tipping investigation. My client had a request from a regulator who provided the names of specific people working in the organization's trading arm and date ranges and asked my client to provide all emails sent or received by those individuals during that date range. There were a lot of people and wide sets of date ranges; we estimated that this would have resulted in a review of millions of records. I estimated I would need 90–100 lawyers to get the review done within the deadline to respond to the regulator. The client was being asked to turn over the documents, but it did not know whether it was the target of the investigation or just providing information being used in another context. The client wanted to know: What could the regulator be looking for? And did we really need to spend millions of dollars on a review if we didn't know specifically what we were looking for? There wasn't much time to do a detailed document-by-document review because there were simply too many documents that would be turned over and we didn't know what keywords to use.

Once upon a time, this would have meant using dozens of junior lawyers to print out and/or review millions of emails—yet we still might not have found anything that showed a connection because we didn't have any context to recognize what we were looking for. I convinced my client to let me use a new system that contained an early form of AI. This technology also had the ability to visualize relationships of communications between people.

We entered all of the emails of the named people and date ranges and used the technology to create a timeline of who was emailing who and when. The preliminary results proved interesting because we noticed a pattern of communications between two people on different teams that ordinarily would not have spoken or emailed with each other. So we were curious, asking ourselves, "Why is person A emailing to person B in another group regularly?" Next, we put companies listed as stock tickers and used these as "keywords" and we plotted out where the communications between these two individuals were on the timeline and then zeroed in on communications made that happened to coincide with specific notable trades. Knowing that the client's investment arm had done a few deals and that one of the individuals might have had access to this information, we also developed searches relating to these specific deals. Pulling all these things together, we did a search and retrieved a subset of emails that we used to train the system. This subset of emails used to train the system also helped us develop a working thesis about why the regulator might be asking after the specific groups of people it was asking about, and what the risk to the organization might be. We used the training set against the balance of the emails that we collected, and instead of reviewing millions of messages, reviewed only the ones the computerized system ranked as higher and more likely to be interesting. We sampled a subset of the records that were not reviewed.

In using this technology, and the workflows it enabled, we saved the client overall many hundreds of thousands of dollars by reviewing only a portion of the total numbers of documents that were ultimately turned over. And the client was able to turn over the emails, understanding that it was not facing any direct risk. The total amount of time it took to do this entire investigation and develop a strategy was materially less than a week, and much of the initial work of finding the training set was done in under a day. The investigation process itself started in the morning, and I finished right before attending a dinner I had that evening, receiving a preliminary report saying, "I think we may want to take a look at this," with the recommended set to review in more detail (i.e., what the AI system ranked to be "of interest"). We finished our investigation of the reviewable items within the week, with the client confident about the submission to be made to the regulator, even though not every email to be turned over was going to be reviewed.

Today, this kind of search and retrieval capability is available within every modern eDiscovery platform, and these applications have become intuitive and easy to use. Almost every large and mid-size law firm in North America, as well as those in the UK, Australia, and New Zealand routinely use this technology, and eDiscovery departments exist within many of those law firms. Additionally, third-party eDiscovery vendors are available. These vendors constitute a multibillion dollar industry. For example, in 2016, OMERS (a Canadian pension fund) bought Epiq, a large eDiscovery technology and services company, in a transaction valued at approximately $1 billion.

eDiscovery technology can not only be used to train a system to retrieve text within documents likely to be responsive, but now have other functionality, such as: the ability to create timelines of who communicated with whom; to pull out and identify proper or place names and put them (and their associated documents) on a map; the ability to annotate, redact, and highlight documents; and the ability to seamlessly move between various document types (i.e., to review a tweet, an email, a text message, and an Excel file all in the same viewer and system). Systems are also emerging to detect "sentiment" (positive or negative feelings being communicated) within email and message communications, to enable human reviewers to focus on communications of emotional interest as categorized by the computer system. The accuracy and reliability of these systems is improving every year.

While the systems are becoming more widely available, the important thing to understand about AI in eDiscovery is that its "learning" is highly fact-specific. A training used in one case is unlikely to be useful in the next case, because the facts and context change from case to case. But, even here, systems are evolving and innovations are emerging such that training on common situations may be imported from one case to another.

Tracking the Next Big Source

Today, many people are communicating through non-text attributes such as video, voice, TikTok, emojis, Instagram, and GIFs, which are resistant to traditional search technologies because these do not involve text and so cannot respond to keywords. So how do we do discovery on those items? How do you search for a specific image, such as "Green Shirt Guy"? This is where innovation in data search techniques will be so important in the coming years, and it is likely that AI will be integrated with these processes.

I worked on a case that turned on the fact that one person sent another person a text with three specific emojis. That one specific person sent another person these exact three emojis was the "a-ha!" moment in the case, the most critical piece of evidence. I didn't find that through a keyword search, because for now, emojis cannot be reliably captured within traditional search mechanisms. In this case, I happened to find this smoking gun mostly manually, by narrowing down and iterating using a search technique on time and location data associated with cell phone records. I was looking at cell phone location data, including time and location of transmission, for information that indicated where these people were moving around. I was using an AI graphing tool to map out where people traveled to see if I could put people together. This case hinged on getting evidence that two people were together off a single cell tower, and then finding that one of them sent a text containing three specific emojis to a third person during that period of time. I did that manually, but I can be confident that shortly an AI will be able to make those connections automatically and highlight that as a possible item for me to look at.

There are multiple types of AI working inside today's eDiscovery technologies. For example, in a single system you might find: text extraction, which makes the texts available; a categorization tool, which puts like things together with like; a searching tool, which helps bring to the surface related items without keywords; and a visualization tool. Each one of these tools is designed to perform a specific role, but they're packaged together and they work together to deliver this experience to the user. eDiscovery is a bit like detective work. The technology improves outcomes and speed, and is fascinating, powerful, and extremely helpful when dealing with today's wealth of information and data sources.

Notes

1. Grossman, M., and G. Cormack. 2011. Technology-Assisted Review in eDiscovery Can Be More Effective and More Efficient Than Exhaustive Manual Review. *The Richmond Journal of Law and Technology* 17 (3).
2. *Moore v. Publicis Groupe,* 287 F.R.D. 182 (S.D.N.Y. 2012).

CHAPTER 8

AI in Legal Research

How AI Is Providing Everyone Access to Information and Leveling the Playing Field for Firms of All Sizes

By Jake Heller, Co-Founder and CEO, Casetext
Laura Safdie, Co-Founder, COO, and General Counsel, Casetext
Pablo Arredondo, Co-Founder and Chief Product Officer, Casetext

Legal research is critical to the practice of law, and artificial intelligence is increasingly critical to legal research. As co-founders of Casetext, a company pushing the boundaries of what artificial intelligence can do in law, we have had a front-row seat to the evolution of this technology and its impact on legal practice. We've watched as our scientists and engineers, as well as our competitors, evolved this technology to where it is today, and we see what's developing "in the lab" that will debut commercially in months or years. In this chapter, we'll share what we've seen so far from this technology and what we expect in the coming years.

But first, let's establish some basics, starting with: what is legal research and why care about it? Fundamentally, legal research is an exercise in determining *what the law is*—information that is then used to advise a client, craft contract language, or persuade a court that it should rule in favor of one party rather than another. Research can make or break a multibillion dollar legal dispute, determine whether someone accused of a crime goes free or to prison, or jeopardize a critical business relationship. Because of its centrality to the practice, lawyers spend nearly one out of every five hours at work researching.[1]

In many countries, including the United States, the task of research is made especially difficult because of the common law system. Under the common law, courts decide disputes on a case-by-case basis, issuing written opinions explaining their rationale. These written opinions become precedent that binds courts going forward. Determining what the law is, therefore, is more complicated than just "looking it up" in a set of rules or guidelines— it requires locating and understanding a rich tapestry of precedents, piecing together (based on how courts ruled in the past) how they will likely decide a particular issue in the future. The problem gets necessarily more complex as time goes on and more precedents are created—both because there are then many more precedents to locate and understand, and also because there are many more precedents that are *not* relevant to a particular situation that might get in the way of finding the answer. There are now well over 10 million court decisions available in most legal research databases comprising hundreds of millions of pages of text. The task of researching within this quantity of information is daunting. Faced with this difficult and growing challenge, legal research has become for many attorneys not only a big drain on their time but something painful they'd rather avoid. And because creating and curating these databases, including critical secondary information, is difficult and costly, legal research tools have traditionally been expensive—often prohibitively expensive to attorneys who represent less monied people and businesses.

Enter artificial intelligence. Artificial intelligence, broadly speaking, is the ability for machines to mimic aspects of human intelligence. The aspect of intelligence particularly applicable to the law is *language*— understanding it (a field called natural language processing) and creating it (natural language generation). Outside of law, we have natural language processing and generation technologies to thank for Google finding the right website based on a simple search, automatic translation of a text from one language to another, and IBM's Watson besting Jeopardy's champions. This field has been studied and worked on to some degree since at least the 1950s. But very recently, machine understanding and generation of text has made exponential leaps, described later on in this chapter, that opens new and exciting possibilities nobody was even dreaming of just a few years ago. These include advancements that have already made research faster, more precise, easier, and less expensive—and therefore accessible to more.

We will look at three ways in which artificial intelligence has influenced legal research: the core search functionality, the creation and curation of the database of information to be searched, and the generation of legal documents—the latter of which we believe will change what "legal research" looks like fundamentally. Finally, we'll explore how the jobs of lawyers and the business of law has already changed in response to these advances in technology.

Can AI Save Lives? The Stakes of Legal Research

Before we dive into the details of the technology and business of artificial intelligence in legal research, it's important to remember what's at stake.

Soon after releasing our first major artificial intelligence product, we got a note from Crawford, a Florida criminal defense attorney. It began: "Casetext literally saved my client's life." He wasn't using the term *literally* hyperbolically. Crawford explained that his client was on trial for a mandatory life sentence. Just as he was gearing up for the trial, his partner left the firm, leaving him to try the case on his own against a team of two prosecutors who would be backed by even more attorneys, legal assistants, investigators, and interns. Crawford explained that without the advantage of artificial intelligence research technology, it would have been difficult or impossible to keep pace with the prosecution as they filed motions critical to the outcome of the trial—determining which witnesses may testify, what evidence is admissible, and which charges should be dismissed. Decisions would have been made in the case detrimental to his client—not because his client was in the wrong, but because the government had more resources. Using advanced technology helped Crawford level the playing field. After a four-day trial, his client was found not guilty.

Still today, years later, we think about Crawford a lot because it's a reminder of what's at stake. The ability of an attorney to research better and faster is not an abstract concept with theoretical benefits. It directly implicates people's livelihood, business, freedom, and, sometimes, lives.

The Dark Times (Before Artificial Intelligence)

Legal research as it exists today began in earnest when legal texts were originally digitized and made into searchable databases, efforts that began nearly 50 years ago. In those early days, the ability to search these databases was crude at best. At first, you would need to know the precise citation for a case or statute to retrieve it—and entering a citation and pulling legal texts was the only form of "legal research" available.

Later, you could search by simple keywords. For example, in a case about whether a car manufacturer should be held liable for a defective air conditioning unit, you could search for documents that contained the words "products liability" and "car" and "air conditioning." But these methods were far too crude. A simple keyword search would bring back thousands of results that included all those words but may have nothing to do with what you're looking for. You might also miss cases where the court, in its decision, used language different from what you searched for ("automobile" or even "truck" or "semi" instead of "car" may still be relevant).

Research systems then introduced increasingly complex but still insufficient methods to filter out the junk. The creation of "terms and connectors" or "Boolean" searches allowed attorneys to do more complex searches. For example, an attorney could enter (car OR automobile) w/100 "products liability" w/p "air conditioning"—requiring the words *car* or *automobile* to be within 100 words of product liability, which must be in the same paragraph as *air conditioning*. This approach came with serious costs. It was difficult to wrangle creating these queries, and even well-trained attorneys would inadvertently design queries that brought in irrelevant material and, worse, unknowingly exclude material that was relevant. And there was still the problem of picking a word for the search that might be different from the words that appear in the precedent most relevant to your research issue.

Things evolved from there, but still in crude ways. Search engines started to enable handcrafted thesauruses, so FMLA would be understood to also search for the "Family Medical Leave Act." And algorithms got better at surfacing more relevant cases, preferencing more recent cases, or cases decided by courts at the appellate level, or cases where the words searched for appear more times more closely together. But the fundamental problems persisted, and, to this day, those using search engines like these often miss critical information while spending most of their time reviewing irrelevant results. No wonder research takes so long!

Search wasn't the only problem. To create a functional database for legal research, it is necessary to include much more than just the text of cases, statutes, and regulations. Critical information like "was this case subsequently overturned?" is something that must be added to the database. It is now near malpractice to research using legal databases without these "citators" that show the links and relationships between cases. Moreover, a lot of helpful information like a summary of the case or the legal issues (often called *headnotes*) the case covers have become standards in legal research. These too must be added to the database.

Without technology to help, these databases of information were created and curated entirely manually—which is to say, thousands upon thousands of people worked on it. Although it may be apocryphal, it was once said that Thomson Reuters's Westlaw and Reed Elsevier's LexisNexis were the largest employers of attorneys in the country—attorneys who would spend all their time adding this information into their respective databases manually.

It's no secret that attorneys are expensive. This practice drove up the costs associated with running a legal research system like Westlaw or LexisNexis, and these costs were passed along to attorneys who have struggled with the high cost of legal research for decades. To this day, there are still thousands of attorneys, most of whom represent less-monied people and organizations, who must go to the public law library to conduct legal research because they simply cannot afford the high costs associated with legal research.

So the time before artificial intelligence made its mark on legal research *sucked*—and today, for the attorneys who use legal research databases that have not fully utilized artificial intelligence, legal research *still sucks*. You pay too much for technology that all too often wastes your time by surfacing irrelevant information while excluding what you're really searching for.

AI in Legal Research Today

Artificial intelligence has made the situation dramatically better. The core problem with older search technologies can be broken down into two deficiencies: *context* and *concepts*. First, the search engines did not have context about what the attorney was working on, a critical piece in retrieving relevant results and omitting irrelevant noise. Second, legal search engines before artificial intelligence searched by keywords instead of *concepts*, which is why it was so common to miss important cases—a court decision may say the same thing you're searching for, but the judge said it using different language. Advancements in contextual, and conceptual, search are made possible because of exciting breakthroughs in natural language processing technology.

The first of these inputs, contextual search, takes a bit of explanation. When doing legal research, what an attorney is working on—their context— *really matters*. Finding precedents relevant to your case means, in practice, finding times when a court has evaluated a situation like yours. Understanding the particularities of your case, and reflecting those details in your legal research, means that the information most relevant to your unique situation can be surfaced to the top. The context of a case is almost necessarily more intricate than what you can fit in a few keywords. That context includes at least the sequence of events that led up to the legal dispute, the parties involved and their organizational or personal particularities, the jurisdiction, and the legal charges levied. Usually, this information spans pages, not keywords, and is contained in documents like a complaint that is filed at the initial stages of the litigation or the various legal briefs that come later.

Until recently, the only way attorneys could communicate their context to a legal research engine was by constructing lengthy keyword queries that invariably led to results that were at once over-inclusive (bringing in irrelevant decisions that happen to include the term) and under-inclusive (missing relevant decisions that happened to use other words to describe the relevant concept). Casetext pioneered a breakthrough in legal research by turning entire legal documents like briefs and pleadings into a form of mega-query.

Casetext's CARA, the first brief-as-query tool brought to market, enabled attorneys to simply drag-and-drop a brief or complaint and effortlessly discover case law relevant to their context.

One of our favorite briefs to demonstrate CARA with was a summary judgment motion filed in a widely followed litigation concerning the employment status of Uber drivers. A group of Uber drivers had filed a class-action lawsuit alleging that they were improperly categorized as independent contractors, and were entitled to the benefits that come with employee status. Uploading this motion into CARA instantly returned a decision from the same court where a judge had denied summary judgment to Lyft on exactly the same claims! Other results centered on other cab drivers, bus drivers, and even FedEx drivers bringing similar claims. Finding all of these cases using traditional tools would have taken a substantial amount of time and one study showed that attorneys missed some of these decisions entirely.

Because adding context to the search experience was so powerful, a lot of legal technology companies have pursued this approach—including Judicata's Clerk, Ross Inteligence's Eva, vLex's Vincent, Westlaw QuickCheck, Lexis Brief Analyzer, and Bloomberg Brief Analyze.

Contextual research is just one of the major advancements in legal search technology. The second, *conceptual searching*, is equally important. Conceptual searching means that the search program "understands" what you are looking for and finds relevant material, even if the language you use to search is dramatically different from the language in the search result. This means that an attorney can search using their own language without fear that they will miss out on a relevant precedent that happens to articulate the same concept differently. For example, a search about "not earning a diploma" might return results regarding "failing to graduate" or "not completing academic training." It also means that the system is less likely to bring back irrelevant results because it won't be fooled by instances where the same words were used but to an entirely different meaning. For example, a query for "patent AND DNA" might return an opinion where a judge wrote, "It is a patent falsehood that prison officials had a warrant to collect a sample of Mr. Smith's DNA." Finally, this form of searching is much easier for the attorney. Instead of using "Boolean" searching logic, the attorney need only write a sentence in their own phrasing (e.g., a sentence for which they would like legal support in a brief), and the system will understand the meaning behind the sentence and use that understanding to find relevant material.

How do machines "understand" sentences? The key breakthrough was Google's 2018 release of a natural language processing technique called BERT (short for "Bidirectional Encoder Representations from Transformers"). Anything resembling a deep dive into BERT is beyond the scope of this chapter, but essentially it overcame some of the limitations that stunted the development of language models (as opposed to other areas of AI like image-recognition). For example, the BERT approach allowed models to be initially trained on enormous volumes of data without the need for resource-intensive human-labeling. Human labeling is now only required for specific fine-tuning tasks that require much less data to work.

Legal texts have a number of domain-specific idiosyncrasies including vocabulary, semantic meaning, and sentence formatting. Considerable work must be done to get these language models to work in a legal context. Even more work, and a few large technical breakthroughs, must be done to make this technology accessible as part of a search application usable by end users instead of in the labs. Given how new this technology is and the difficulty involved in making it work well in a legal context, only a handful of legal technology companies have brought this technology to market as of this writing. Casetext is to our knowledge the only company that has released a full-fledged legal research engine based on the BERT approach (released as a tool called "Parallel Search"). The early response has been overwhelmingly positive, which is unsurprising given how often attorneys need to find conceptual matches to a query. LexisNexis's latest platform upgrade, Lexis+, has a question and answer feature called Lexis Answers that is advertised as being driven by BERT technology.

Contextual search and conceptual search are not mutually exclusive technologies; rather, they are most powerful when combined. Search technologies that take into account the context of the specific litigation an attorney is working on while also searching for concepts rather than keywords represent the best-in-class artificial intelligence search technologies.

Besides these technologies, which are search applications, artificial intelligence has also reduced the expense associated with creating and curating legal research databases—and ultimately has helped make legal research more affordable and accessible to more attorneys. As described above, legal research databases contain far more than just the law itself, but also information that makes legal research efficient and easy. For years, that information was curated manually by thousands of attorneys. Today, artificial intelligence technologies are doing more and more of the heavy lifting, reducing the labor requirements and associated expenses while enabling the attorneys to review and work on the most difficult and pressing tasks beyond the capabilities of artificial intelligence technologies.

Take, for example, the warnings legal research databases contain that indicate whether a precedent has been subsequently overturned—a feature in LexisNexis called "Shepard's," in Westlaw called "KeyCite," and in Casetext called "SmartCite." There are hundreds of millions of instances of cases citing previous cases, and reviewing each of these relationships manually would take centuries. For example, LexisNexis's Shepard's feature was born out of a manual effort, where each case relationship was meticulously recorded by hand and published in many volumes of books, that began in the 1800s.

Natural language processing technologies have made this process considerably more achievable on a shorter timescale and with fewer people.

These technologies can find language that likely indicates that one case overruled another, and flag that for human review, confidently and at a high level of precision saying that the remaining relationships do not represent one case overturning another. One thing we found fascinating was the "features" (words/phrases) our NLP systems found predictive of a case being overruled. For example, the word *today* was suggestive as judges, perhaps in a bit of fanfare, would often announce that they "today" render an earlier holding obsolete. There were many more examples where the machine taught the lawyers about patterns we never would have guessed.

By taking centuries of rote work out of the process of creating and curating the legal research database, legal research becomes more affordable for two reasons: First, as the costs for creating legal research databases go down, those cost savings are passed on to the attorneys that subscribe to these services. Second, creating a legal research database has become substantially more achievable by newer startup companies that are creating a truly competitive environment with the older, legacy providers that have enjoyed near-monopoly status for decades. Casetext, for example, is approximately a third of the cost of the larger competitors, one key reason over 6,500 law firms have joined the platform over the last two years.

Thanks to artificial intelligence, today's attorneys can find better information faster while paying less. Even more exciting is what's on the horizon.

AI BY ANY OTHER NAME

By Noah Waisberg and Dr. Alexander Hudek

Artificial intelligence often turns up in places where users don't necessarily know they are using AI. Often, that's because AI-based features often come to products that users are already using for specific purposes, and the AI operates in the background, without any extra actions or knowledge required from the users. Legal research is one such area.

The legal research space has been dominated by a few commercial vendors, including Thomson Reuters and LexisNexis. A look at the history of the development of Thomson Reuters' Westlaw research service provides plenty of illustrative examples of how AI has infiltrated the legal research space, often under the radar of lawyers who don't realize they are using AI. Here is a brief timeline:

- In 1992, before Google was a household name for its search engine, Westlaw introduced Westlaw Is Natural (WIN), the first commercial search engine featuring probabilistic rank retrieval. Users now had the ability to enter natural language searches rather than only using Boolean search connectors like AND, OR, NOT.

- In 2000 Westlaw introduced "entity extraction" capabilities called People-Cite and Profiler. These features used machine learning to extract personal names from case law and link those names to other works associated with those names (such as articles).

- The Westlaw system leverages the work of hundreds of attorney-editors, who classify points of law in court decisions and write summaries of them. Behind the scenes, AI helps those editors. Starting in 2001, Thomson Reuters has used machine learning algorithms to assist with the classification of court decisions into Westlaw's taxonomy of law (called the Key Number System).

- That system evolved into ResultsPlus, which was a user-facing application of the same technology. For a given search in the core case law database, Westlaw would leverage machine learning algorithms to make recommendations to users of relevant secondary sources such as articles or treatises.

- A major upgrade of Westlaw came with the introduction of WestlawNext in 2010. This new version of Westlaw leveraged an array of AI-based capabilities, including machine learning (ML), clustering, classification, usage log analysis, citation network analysis, topic modeling, and natural language generation. This was a major step forward but, as with the previous innovations, the features were simply built into an existing tool; users did not need to know they were using AI.

- In 2018, Westlaw was revamped again under the name Westlaw Edge, and this time three distinct AI-based innovations were part of the release:

1. *WestSearch Plus*. Answers questions posed in plain language. Rather than simply returning a list of documents relevant to the question, it provides an actual answer derived from the editorial work of Westlaw editors and machine learning and natural language processing techniques.

2. *Litigation Analytics*. Allows lawyers to predict outcomes by mining past court dockets for insights about judges, parties, courts, and areas of law. It leverages visualization techniques and uses AI to extract and normalize data from thousands of courts.

3. *KeyCite Overruling Risk*. An AI-based enhancement to Westlaw's citator system, KeyCite expanded the scope of citation analysis in case law. Previously, KeyCite could only flag cases where a court had explicitly overruled a previous case. With Overruling Risk, KeyCite uses machine learning techniques to identify cases that are overruled implicitly, for example, when a case that it relied on as precedent was itself overruled.

- In 2019, Westlaw introduced Quick Check, a document analysis tool. Users can upload a full brief or other legal document and the system will automatically suggest other case law authorities that are relevant to the document but not cited in it.

Richard Punt, chief strategy officer of Thomson Reuters, says, "AI has played a central role in our approach to legal research for many years. Combined with our editorial capabilities and expertise in content structuring, it has helped lawyers find better answers, more efficiently. Our dedicated Center for Cognitive Computing reflects that sustained commitment. As machine learning continues to advance, we see significant further opportunities to develop our research tools, blending the artificial with the human."

If you ask an ordinary person if they are big users of AI, most would likely say no. The AI they use in products like their smartphones, the ecommerce site where they shop, or in the apps where they stream music or video, is largely invisible to them. They don't have to choose to use it; it's just part of the product. It's the same with legal research; for decades now, AI techniques have made their way into legal research products, and lawyers have been leveraging that technology, often without being conscious that it's AI.

AI Will Help to Write the Future

To us, the most exciting application of legal research will be coming in the next few years. These applications will be different in one substantial way: rather than just helping attorneys find information to add to a brief or other legal document, they will be helping attorneys write those documents.

Most legal research is done with the intention of deploying that information researched in a handful of ways: most commonly, to advise a client, strategize regarding whether a lawsuit can be pursued, or write a legal brief to persuade a court that your position is backed by precedent. In each of these cases, there is usually associated written work product, like a memorandum or brief. We anticipate that the most exciting applications of artificial intelligence will skip the step of research and go directly to aiding an attorney write work product that automatically and correctly identifies the right precedent.

Today, the field of natural language generation is just starting to show real signs of promise. For example, the technology company OpenAI released a new algorithm, GPT3, that writes convincing-sounding language when given a prompt—including legal language. The technology is eerily good at writing language that appears on the surface indistinguishable from something written by a human.[2] But technologies like GPT3 are still in the early stages of development; in the legal context, algorithms like this might *sound* like a lawyer wrote it but get the substance completely wrong.

It is unlikely that machines will ever truly do the writing for lawyers—there is too much knowledge, strategy, and persuasion built into legal writing. But they can assist substantially. In the not-too-distant future, for example, a lawyer may write out the factual circumstances of the case and a machine process will suggest the legal arguments available to the attorney, the cases and other legal authorities they can cite, and some starter language to begin writing out the legal argument. Another example would be a much more advanced "autocomplete" feature for legal writing, where an attorney begins a thought and the computer suggests what is most likely going to be said next along with corresponding legal authorities to back it up.

In these sorts of examples, what is known today as *legal research*—searching through a database of legal authorities to find relevant precedents and other materials—is turned on its head. Instead of the focus being on searching, the focus becomes on the final written work product. And the attorney does barely any searching at all in this new world. Rather, the attorney focuses on the heart of the craft—framing the facts of the case, choosing the arguments they will pursue, and writing persuasively—and the system provides the research or at least suggestions that the attorney can validate and add if appropriate.

A future without legal research as it is currently known may seem far off to many attorneys, but the beginnings of this work is happening today. For example, Compose, a new product we have been working on, already suggests all common legal arguments and legal authorities for a growing number of legal issues that an attorney can add to the language of their brief with one click. And when Compose has not covered a legal issue, the contextual and conceptual search technologies described above enable an attorney to find legal support for any sentence they write. These technologies represent the first step toward a dramatically more efficient (and enjoyable) research and writing process for attorneys.

AI Will Continue to Help Lawyers Do Higher Value Work

With the introduction of new technologies to the legal profession, especially those that automate or make easier some aspects of legal practice, there is always some amount of understandable consternation—will these technologies take away the attorney's autonomy, the more fulfilling aspects of practice, or job?

On the contrary, these advances in technology are already changing for the better what it means to be a lawyer and law firm. As artificial intelligence becomes better at locating the best precedents and avoiding irrelevant material, lawyers are shifting their time to higher-value and more rewarding tasks, like strategizing, writing persuasively, and investigating the facts of the case. Because the work is much more efficient, law firms are finding friendlier ways to bill for their services, including charging a flat fee rather than charging by the hour. Where in the past there was a real advantage to having an army of associates research a topic—which benefited larger firms and the well-financed clients who could afford them—modern technologies enable a single attorney to quickly find the most relevant precedents and produce high-quality work product, in effect leveling the playing field. And as legal work becomes increasingly efficient and predictable, the attorneys can represent clients who are not well-resourced and do so at the highest level of practice.

In short, we see a future of legal practice that is more efficient, just, and fulfilling—which is why we do what we do.

Notes

1. American Bar Association. 2019. Legal Technology Survey 2019—Online Research (explaining that lawyers spend on average 17% of their time researching); Steve Lastres, LLRX Report: Rebooting Legal Research in a Digital Age (2013) https://www.llrx.com/2013/08/rebooting-legal-research-in-a-digital-age/ (finding that younger attorneys spend more than 30% of their time conducting legal research).
2. If you want to see examples, a website has compiled them: https://gpt3examples.com/

CHAPTER 9

Litigation Analytics

The Emergence of Analytics in Law and Why It's Now Dangerous to Practice Litigation Without Data

By Anthony Niblett, Co-Founder of Blue J Legal
Associate Professor, University of Toronto Faculty of Law

Law is a competitive profession and operating at an informational disadvantage can be costly. This is nothing new; through the nineteenth and much of the twentieth century, you would be at a competitive disadvantage if you didn't have access to legal books. In the late 1990s and early in the 2000s, you were at a disadvantage if you didn't have access to a Westlaw or Lexis CD ROM. In the 2010s, you were at a disadvantage if you didn't have access to Westlaw or Lexis online. Today—and going forward—you will have an informational disadvantage if you don't have access to predictive tools that can help you sift through vast amounts of information and help provide the most relevant data, because—let's face it—there's a ton of information out there.

There is a lot of law. And some of these laws are extraordinarily complex. The cases are voluminous and the statutes or regulations can be dense. No lawyer can have extensive knowledge on every area of law. This can create an enormous problem: a lack of clarity. Too much information may make it very difficult to determine clearly what the law is. When you try to determine what the law is, the following questions lie in the back of your mind: What happens if your client has a dispute with somebody and that dispute goes to court? In order to best serve your client, you need to know what the law says and what would happen if your client's dispute was to go before a judge or an arbitrator. How would this case most likely be resolved? How can you find the best information to resolve the case in favor of your client?

Lawyers need to make predictions about the likely outcomes of disputes. Typically, lawyers have relied on their knowledge of the law, along with their intuition, to make highly educated guesses about how the court will resolve a dispute. But in recent years, lawyers have started to use data-driven AI tools to help make these predictions. An example may prove helpful. Imagine your client is a business that hires workers. She is unsure whether to characterize these workers as employees of the company or as independent contractors. Classifying workers correctly is important for many legal reasons. This legal issue is central to questions of tax liability, employment obligations, and tort law (generally, your client can be held vicariously liable for their employees' actions, but generally not for the actions of independent contractors). It's important for questions of pensions, payroll tax, and for insurance. The miscategorization of workers, which on the surface may appear to be just one narrow legal issue, can lead to millions of dollars' worth of fines or a class action suit against your client. Problematically, this is an extremely vague area of law, since there's no single bright line test that provides a simple answer as to whether an individual is definitely an independent contractor or definitely an employee. There are so many potential factors and variables that make the legal issue vague and fuzzy. As a result, there have been hundreds or thousands of cases investigating how hiring firms have classified their workers. Often, the litigation dispute involves enterprises that believe their workers are independent contractors, but the court investigates whether, given all the circumstances, the relationship was one of employer-employee.

Cases like this come up all of the time and new rulings in a court may change the answer as to how to classify a worker. Let's say you had a case in which, based on your knowledge of relevant cases, you told your client that the truck drivers working for them should be classified as independent contractors. However, suppose that a month ago a court handed down a ruling that changes the interpretation of the law here, and suggested that the truck drivers working for your client are actually employees. Having gone ahead and classified them incorrectly, based on an outdated understanding of the case law, your client would now be liable for fines for mischaracterizing their workers and for unpaid taxes.

Lawyers need to make these types of predictions all the time. And the predictions need to be accurate. Should you fight this, or should you settle? Should your client take a plea bargain? Is a tax-saving structure legal? Has your client actually used "reasonable best efforts"? You need to know what the most recent and applicable laws are (and what the court rulings have been) for your client's specific situation in order to give the best advice. You need the right data to provide the right answers.

Why Am I the Right Person to Discuss Litigation Analytics?

As a law professor, trained as an economist, the predictability of legal outcomes is a topic that has intrigued me for some time. A lot of my academic research has centered on judicial biases and judicial inconsistency. I study how statistics can be used to analyze the law. I ask the following types of questions:

1. Can we use statistics to describe the law?
2. Can we use statistics to explain the law?
3. Can we use statistics to predict the law and what will happen in the next case that will come to court?

Today, I use my background in statistics to work with both the legal research and data science teams at Blue J Legal, a legal tech company in Toronto, Canada, that I co-founded. I work with the team that generates data sets used to make predictions about what will happen in future legal cases, should the disputes come to court.

Research, Data, and Predictions: Pre- and Post-AI

Before the development of AI predictive tools, if you were a lawyer engaged in litigation, you would typically research by finding the most relevant cases that fit your needs. Take the example of classifying truck drivers as employees or independent contractors. You might start by doing an online search for cases that involve this narrow legal issue. The problem isn't finding cases; you'll find many of them—far more than you need. You may try to narrow the search by looking for cases that involve truck drivers. You may return a number of cases about taxi drivers, pizza delivery drivers, and so forth. Perhaps you narrow it down to the five most relevant cases. They may be about drivers but these drivers' situations may differ from your particular situation in important ways. For example, these drivers may be working under a different type of contract, may not own the relevant assets, or they may have fewer degrees of freedom. The drivers in the precedents may or may not be setting their own schedules or wearing uniforms. Do these distinctions make a difference? How much of a difference? If you just focus on those five cases that you pulled from your research, you may do yourself (and your client) a great disservice. You may not be getting a complete picture of the law.

You will, therefore, have to research more broadly to find specific cases with similar contracts, asset ownership, control, and other specifics that closely match those of your truck drivers. To accomplish this, you may need to spend hours and hours trying to read through cases. You'll look for cases you may have missed, trying to find important cases that will help you determine the answer.

Basically, legal research has traditionally involved a lot of grunt work. Lawyers need to carefully read through cases trying to be sure they're not missing anything. They have to research broadly, relying on legal research software to help.

After reviewing the cases, you would write up a memo distilling the relevant rules and explaining how they apply to your client's case. The memo would typically make a prediction about how a court would rule if the case were to be litigated. The memo would further outline the reasons—what factors would be most important here and examining how courts have weighed the different factors in previous cases.

Legal research takes time. And it is costly. Those costs get pushed onto the client and, increasingly, they do not want to pay for all of that, especially the hours of research. They've come to a lawyer who is supposedly an expert, and they expect you to know the answer. You've given them a memo, and they say, "Well, how come this is costing me so much?" So, you explain: "Well, we had to do 20 hours of research. We had to get Jim and Jill out there researching every single case, reading every single case, trying to find the right answer, and writing up the memo, making sure that they didn't miss anything. That's why this process costs so much money." And, compounding matters, no matter how many cases the team is able to read, there are hundreds or thousands more cases on the topic that were not read.

Artificial intelligence can help. AI tools have been developed that can give you more immediate answers. Answers can be provided at a vastly reduced cost. AI can search through all pertinent cases on the issue at hand and then locate those that are closest to the facts of your client's case. It can provide clear information about how courts have resolved the most relevant, and recent, disputes, and how they will likely do so in the future. It allows lawyers to make clear predictions regarding how a court would resolve a particular dispute.

AI can identify which factors and variables are the most important. Let's return to our worker classification example. The AI tools may, hypothetically, find the data shows that if you are giving your drivers a lot of freedom to create and maintain their schedules, that makes them statistically far more likely to be categorized as independent contractors. It may show you that the fact that you make them wear a uniform is insignificant, but the fact that they own their truck is super important.

This is letting the data speak. It is not the lawyer using their judgment about what is important. It is simply a distillation of what courts have decided over the course of hundreds or thousands of cases. By letting the data speak, you save on research time. AI can give you a more complete answer, by taking into account every single case that's gone to court on this particular issue. The algorithms can determine how much weight courts are likely to place on each individual factor in a given case. It's no longer just a judgment skill; now you can use AI algorithms to give you the most likely potential outcomes: this is what courts have done in the past, and this is how they're most likely to decide in the future.

The AI can also provide reasons for the predictions in the form of a memo. After identifying which factors are most important, AI can determine what text to put into the memo. In the end, it can produce a memo that stipulates: "For the following reasons, it is 80% likely that the court would classify the truck drivers as independent contractors."

THE MAP AND THE TERRITORY (*WHY GOOD LEGAL DATA MATTERS*)

By Joshua Walker, Co-Founder of Lex Machina and CodeX (Stanford Center for Legal Informatics); Author of *On Legal AI*

US Supreme Court Justice Louis Brandeis wrote: "Sunlight is said to be the best of disinfectants; electric light the most efficient policeman."[1] It is a familiar adage to most US attorneys, often learned in the early days of law school. And while Brandeis was talking about the press, it applies equally to what we use artificial intelligence for in the law: illuminating problems and performance. It is serving this function for practitioners, governments, the press, and citizens. Well-crafted legal AI, and the data it reveals, can help detect and avoid civic problems like potholes under a street lamp. It can help attorneys and legal systems alike improve performance.

Most people experience the law as a kind of dark thicket . . . a crowd of thorns they blunder into in the middle of the night. No wonder so many people don't like attorneys.

The law should not be an impenetrable maze. It should be a light switch. It should entail a simple interface that anyone can use to illuminate the room.

Here is a real-life example. In 2011, the United States enacted a law dubbed the "America Invents Act." In it, Congress asked the General Accountability Office (essentially the chief auditor for the US government) to study so-called "patent trolls" / patent monetization entities. At the time, I had recently led a company called Lex Machina out of Stanford's Law School and AI Lab. Lex Machina focused on IP and other litigation data (not doctrine, directly; data about all filings, all motions, and all outcomes, judges, lawyers, etc.). We competed fiercely for the opportunity to provide the GAO with empirical data. We successfully argued that we could provide the cleanest data (i.e., most objective and comprehensive data) to support them. Both sides of the patent debates disliked elements of the GAO report that eventually came out (which is a good sign). But here is what they actually found, if I can be pardoned for oversimplification: (a) "patent troll" is a rhetorical term that does not necessarily map to a clearly and convincingly harmful legal entity category; and (b) the US was *terrible* at creating software patents—the vast majority of software patents asserted in court get invalidated, at least in part. When anomalies like that get illuminated, it gets easier for advocates and judges to fix them. Contemporaneously, judges and policy makers sharpened standards for not only software patents, but also for patent damages, jurisdiction, and other core IP system elements. It is impossible to attribute a single cause to any one of those judicial, legislative, or executive branch decisions. But we believe clean, legally accurate data helps catalyze not only initial adjustments, but ongoing optimization over time: both for actors within those systems (client outcomes) and systems as a whole. In short, legal "history" helps us create better outcomes and avoid the mistakes of the past.

Before empirical illumination of those patent lawsuits, lobbyists and appellate attorneys were like people trying to rearrange someone's living room in the dark. No one knew where the furniture *was*, much less what the optimal legal configuration would be. Now—for all our undoubtedly many policy flaws—we can at least argue about real things, real data . . . not shadows. And we can do this for more important domains, like criminal and constitutional law as well. (Again, I mean this in a very specific way. For example, if the data shows that the median criminal sentences for crack cocaine possession are 100 times longer than for powdered cocaine, and the possession types map to race, it is a reason for the courts and Congress to reevaluate and intervene. The data can help us humanize and improve social outcomes. They should never be used to dehumanize, or replace judgments better developed by judges.) Legally precise artificial intelligence is essential for extracting actionable intelligence out of very large and/or complex data sets. Purely manual expert efforts will drown in data before producing results. Legally naïve, pure engineering approaches will wash out legal nuance, and may materially diverge from accurate, useful conclusions.

A traditional law school curriculum teaches you to think, analyze, argue, and write at a higher level. It teaches you, speaking analogously, about the "laws of physics." But your clients want to—again analogously (if sometimes literally)—build airplanes and fly places. You need to teach them about flight physics to some extent, yes, but also and particularly about (i) the map, (ii) air traffic, and (iii) ultimately, optimal routing. Lawyers are taught to be good legal "scientists," but our clients need to get from X to Y in an optimal manner. There is a disconnect.

Empirical litigation (and other) legal data classes can provide a kind of living map that tells clients where they are and that helps them do flight planning. The next generation of legal AI tools will help them build better "airplanes." We will also optimize legal vehicles for live conditions.

Leveraging AI, we can illuminate the territory for clients, and also help improve systems.

LEX MACHINA AND THE RISE OF LITIGATION ANALYTICS

By Noah Waisberg and Dr. Alexander Hudek

In 2006, lawyers relied on their own expertise and experience to make decisions about questions such as whether to pursue a case, how much to settle for, how to budget for a certain case duration, what to expect from a certain judge, and so forth.

That started to change as a handful of academic institutions started looking into analyzing the data behind the legal system. Stanford University eventually developed one of the leading centers for research on the use of computing in law: CodeX, the Stanford Center for Legal Informatics, which was founded in 2008 as a partnership between the Law School and the Department of Computer Science.

CodeX has been more than a center for academic research in legal informatics; because of its unique position in Silicon Valley it has also spawned a number of legal technology startups through its network of scientists, engineers, lawyers, law students, entrepreneurs, and venture capitalists.

An early attempt to marry data to legal practice was Lex Machina. The origin of the company in 2006 was professor Mark Lemley's simple question: "Where is the best place to file a patent case?" Lemley teamed up with colleagues at Stanford and lawyer Joshua Walker to build a database of information about every patent case filed in the US. In 2010, Lex Machina was formed as a private company to develop the project into a commercial venture. Seed funding was raised, and law firms and corporate legal departments signed up as customers.

Lex Machina's first product was Legal Analytics, a platform that allowed lawyers to analyze data about past court cases in order to make decisions about current cases. The system was built on a massive effort to read, clean, and tag millions of docket entries—the public records of every step in a court case, including initial complaints, responses, motions, and judicial decisions. It also collected the metadata around all that data, including dates, dollar amounts, subject matter, and relationships between parties, judges, and lawyers.

With all that data collected in an analytical platform, lawyers could now answer questions about federal court cases: How long does this type of case typically last? What is this law firm's success rate before this judge? What is this judge's likelihood of granting this type of motion? How often has this party been engaged in this type of case? What are typical damage awards for this type of case? All of these are questions that had been asked of and answered by lawyers in the past, but now they could have solid data driving their responses.

The offering was successful enough that it was acquired in 2015 by legal information giant LexisNexis, and it has continued to expand in scope, first into other areas of federal courts litigation. More recently, it has begun to launch offerings built on state court docket data, expanding the service into new practice areas. Today Lex Machina is used by 74% of the AmLaw 100 firms.

Other players have entered the space. LexisNexis' rival Thomson Reuters built an analytics offering, Westlaw Litigation Analytics, on top of its existing dockets product. Bloomberg Law also developed an analytics offering, and another offering, Docket Alarm, was acquired by legal research provider Fastcase in 2018. Niche markets have developed; Blue J Legal provides a predictive analytics platform targeted to the tax law space.

Today, the idea of using data and analytics to enhance legal decision-making is no longer novel. Support for data-driven decision-making is at the heart of many technology-based products in legal research, contract analysis, eDiscovery, and law firm management. An entire industry's approach to data has shifted.

So, How Does It Actually Work?

The foundation for these types of litigation prediction tools is the raw data contained in judicial opinions. The text of legal opinions is freely available in comprehensive, extensive databases that have been collated over the course of many years. There is considerable manual effort in turning these unstructured written opinions into a structured dataset. At Blue J, we structure our data around particular legal issues (e.g., is a worker an independent contractor or an employee?). This requires us to find all the relevant cases on a particular issue and then create a structured dataset of the merits of these decisions.

You, as the user, enter the facts of your client's case into the software. The AI then compares the facts of your client's case to every single case that has gone to court on this issue. Our machine learning algorithms then determine how much weight courts have placed on each of these factors. These weights are not static; they are not the same in every case. Not unlike a detective on a difficult case, the more pertinent information you provide, the more AI can compare your specific case information to that of other cases and home in on the most appropriate, similar case results.

The AI tools can compare the facts of your client's case to every other case that has gone to court. The AI can then predict an outcome—given how courts have resolved these disputes in the past, how will they likely resolve your client's case? For example, the prediction may be that if the case goes to court, it is 80% likely that a court would find this to be an independent contractor.

OUTRUNNING YOUR COMPETITORS

By Joshua Walker

Data can level the playing field and rapidly increase comparative or local knowledge for folks who previously had to guess, or hire local counsel, for the same (or inferior) data. For example, I once had a major client who was pitching a new patent case in Georgia. He knew nothing about the judge beforehand, and had never practiced there before. Ordinarily, he might not have pitched it, or he might have at least hired a local partner before pitching the case.

Instead, he used AI tools (empirical data) and came in prepared, knowing everything this judge had done, every major motion she had granted or denied. He had her appeal record, her judgments, and much more. The client hired him. This attorney was retained based on his own merit. But the data empowered him. This case was representative, and he was also able to regularly use empirical data to (i) optimize motion filings (avoiding nonessential motions that were unlikely to win) and (ii) budget.

At a major technology corporation, a veteran in house counsel wanted to hire one law firm over another. She knew in her gut that the former firm was likely to perform better; but the latter firm was substantially cheaper. The in house counsel argued for the more expensive counsel to the head of finance. But Finance asked the obvious question: "How much better could they really be?" Using empirical litigation data and careful interpretation, the General Counsel's office actually showed the Finance Department how much better the expensive lawyer was (something they felt they already knew but couldn't prove). Essentially, a company's lawyers can say: "Here are the cases they've taken," considering difficulty, etc., and show how they fared in each one. This can provide a value delta for a particular class of law firm.

In this case, value didn't mean the cheaper firm. It meant the one that delivered better results, net of their cost, to the corporation.

More generally, expert application of legal empirical data, legal history (as extracted by good legal AI; more on this later) can bridge a gap between legal and finance. Legal can finally communicate qualitative nuance to a quantitative domain—finance—to the measurable benefit of the corporation.

It is not as if empirical data tells you *why* a lawyer is good. It *can* demonstrate that phenomenon, and its business impact. And that is why it is a competitive advantage to lawyers pitching cases, transactions, and strategy. It enables lawyers to translate legal outcomes into business and finance contexts—and thereby be more successful in enterprise and financial institutions.

Impacting Lawyers

Litigation analytics tools are changing lawyers' worlds. Spending less time researching for any given matter means that lawyers can take on additional capacity and they can work out alternative fee arrangements with clients. But it's more than that. These tools help lawyers get the robust data they need and get it more quickly. While legal research software—AI-powered or not—gets lawyers the right cases, legal prediction software tries to go one step further: figuring out what all the information means. This means lawyers can let clients know where they stand early in the process and how much more time they expect they will need to spend on the case. Clients are then able to make an informed decision. If, for example, the software predicts that a case could go either way—in other words, it indicates that there is only a 55% chance that the ruling would be in favor of the client—the lawyer could explain that their legal team will have to do significant work on that matter in order to get to a position that could be strongly argued in favor of the client. On the flip side, if the lawyer received a matter that indicated that their client is 95% likely to have a ruling in their favor, they would most likely not need to sink more resources into developing their position. This goes back to what we said earlier about clarity: AI provides a clearer picture of how the process will likely unfold.

The other thing that litigation analysis AI really helps lawyers do is organize their data. Lawyers often have a lot of scattered ways of documenting their due diligence, but using AI provides a nice way of centralizing a lot of the core thinking that went into the background of each matter. The report feature found on most litigation analytics software allows you to see exactly how you're thinking about each of the questions posed by the questionnaire. Once again, the data, and even the process, is easily available and transparent. There's a pretty rigorous and robust research process that you can document and then show clients if your position is contested.

The Future of AI Litigation Software

As legal software permeates the industry, litigation analytics tools will be used in more law firms but could be used by courts and arbitrators as well. As a result, the proportion of settlements will increase, because both sides will have the same information. They will be on the same page. In the employment law context, for example, we have seen how lawyers use these predictive tools to arrive at settlement. In determining how much severance pay a dismissed worker should be paid, the lawyers for the employer and former employee typically disagree about what is "reasonable." But there are thousands and thousands of cases showing what courts hold to be reasonable in different circumstances. We have observed situations where both the employer's lawyers and the employee's lawyers have used our prediction software. Initially, the two parties' positions were quite far apart, but when both used the software, the range of disagreement was vastly reduced. Indeed, we have heard of settlement meetings where both sides have turned up to the meeting with a Blue J report. This type of information facilitates easier settlement as the two parties are disagreeing about fewer things.

Therefore, as these prediction tools continue to develop, you will see more settlement of disputes and fewer cases going to court. Less litigation means lower costs for clients. But if you take it one step further: it's not only that there will be less litigation, there will also be fewer disputes. If everyone knows how courts will resolve potential disputes, the likelihood of a dispute arising will be greatly reduced. This, ultimately, solves the problems associated with a lack of clarity. That's the big picture.

We've entered an era of high-level legal analytics; legal research is becoming increasingly *computational*. Firms are now starting to adopt these AI tools. In the very near future, not having access to tools like AI will become a severe disadvantage. Better information leads to better predictions. And better predictions lead to better performance as a lawyer, at far lower cost.

People often ask me if I, as a law professor, am concerned that these types of predictive tools will replace the jobs of human lawyers that I have trained throughout the years. I am not. AI will not replace lawyers. But lawyers who use AI will replace lawyers who don't.

Note

1. Brandeis, L. D. 1914. *Other People's Money and How the Bankers Use It*. New York: Frederick A. Stokes Company. Originally published in *Harper's Weekly* in "What Publicity Can Do," December 20, 1913, p. 10.

CHAPTER 10

Contract Review to Contract Capital

How Ubiquitous Access to Contract Analysis Software Will Transform Legal and Business Practices

C ontracts are perhaps the most important documents in the world in terms of their impact and governance on all of our fundamental business relationships. They include much more than what most people perceive as the traditional parts of a legal agreement. A vast amount of important details can be found in them—all of a company's business relationships with customers, suppliers, investors, regulators, and employees. Think about a company that has hundreds of thousands or millions of contracts. It's a wealth of information. It's their contract capital.

Understanding the details of your contracts offers a tremendous opportunity. For one, it helps businesses make better decisions. Remember HP's acquisition of Autonomy for $11.7 billion? Because of due diligence problems (including limited contract review), it took an $8.8 billion write-down on the deal within a year. Or AIG, which at the time was the leading insurance company in the United States, but had to be bailed out by the federal government and broken up, primarily because it did not understand the risky contracts it was writing in one small corner of its ginormous business.

Contracts also protect companies from changes in the world and new regulations that keep coming at a faster pace. When the disruptions caused by COVID-19 struck, plenty of businesses needed to know ASAP whether a pandemic counted as an event of force majeure under their contracts or which of their contracts they could cheaply terminate in a desperate dash to cut costs. How does a company quickly adapt its contracts and legal requirements to modifications in IFRS, or Dodd–Frank, or LIBOR (which is estimated to impact an estimated $370 trillion of global financial contracts)? Or new and evolving regulations, like the EU's General Data Protection Regulation? Contract understanding—supported by efficient and accurate contract review—is a company's best way to manage through changing times.

What's holding us back? Why is it that for most organizations, it isn't possible to access, manage, or make sense of their most valuable information, or do it at the pace of competitive business today? Why can't they take on *more* calculated risk?

The answer is the traditional review process—the manual review of documents without the support of computer automation. In this old model of behavior, important information is inevitably missed and therefore becomes a roadblock to operating efficiently and intelligently. Therefore, most businesses (of all sizes) have no clue what is included in the vast majority of their contracts. Even many of the most sophisticated companies in the world don't know what more than 10% of their contracts say. We know because we asked a number of them. Many executives don't know why negotiating provisions matter, nor do they know what impact they could have during or after a transaction. They don't know which of their contracts they can terminate for convenience, which has an automatic inflation-based price increase built-in, and where they have limited protection from a limitation of liability clause. These are things they should know but don't because the cost of finding the answer is too high. It can take one to five minutes a page to review a contract, and, even at low-cost-jurisdiction rates, that can add up fast. For M&A transactions and the like, many companies will simply do a standard "material contract" review, which we talked about in Chapter 2. However, AI now allows much deeper insight with manageable timelines and prices.

Daimler, the automotive company that did a major restructuring (discussed in Chapter 2) illustrates what it means to do more law in order to get a thorough understanding of the business by reviewing millions of contracts. It also suggests how a company can better comprehend the risks in their business today and how they can take more calculated risks in the future because they have a deeper understanding of all their business relationships. It's so important for a company to actually know the status of each contractual relationship, as opposed to guessing or assuming, as they might do now.

It's also important to remember that technology does not just work on its own; it works in conjunction with the people using it. Once the system has reviewed the documents it may go to humans for further review and analysis or there may be a need to add more questions to the process by training the AI. Additional questions can lead to a deeper review process. In other cases, the lawyers or legal team may be relying more heavily on technology. Since contract analysis can serve many purposes, the number of people involved in the process can vary significantly. The goal of contract review is to provide clients with a more in-depth picture of their business relationships and have the ability to make key decisions based on what they have found in the contracts. Such findings can work to the client's advantage.

Contract analysis is not the oldest tool in the legal AI spectrum but it was one of the first and has emerged as one of the most significant. The introduction of contract analysis has reshaped the way corporate lawyers go about their work and the manner in which companies make decisions. To the delight of junior associates, AI has minimized their need to review contracts, allowing them to take on tasks more commensurate with their law school training and high billable rates.

WHY ME?

By Noah Waisberg

I've been involved in automated contract review for over a decade. In fact, when I started down this road, Donald Trump was still a reality TV host. I had done and supervised my fair share of contract reviews as a corporate associate at Weil, Gotshal & Manges, a large and well regarded New York City headquartered law firm. I knew there had to be a better way to do contract reviews, and with my partner and co-author, Alex, we built it through the use of AI.

Roughly a decade into running Kira Systems, I can say without hesitation that AI has significantly changed the process of contract review and will continue to do so. Am I biased? Sure, but I've seen the actual results from numerous tests and heard from *many* customers. AI makes a major difference. It's almost akin to the difference between driving a Tesla and the Flintstones' car.

What's Wrong with Traditional Software-Free Contract Review?

Currently, most contract review is still conducted by junior lawyers without the benefit of technology. They take the first crack at reviewing the contracts, typically looking for set information (e.g., in an M&A transaction, what happens on assignment and change of control under a target company's agreements; in a contract management database population exercise, items the company chooses to track, such as agreement duration, payment terms, insurance provisions, and much more). They then put their findings into summary charts. These charts take different forms, including organized lists of verbatim clauses, summarized provisions, and answers to questions.

Senior people, such as mid-level associates at large law firms, often then spot-check the first level review results. Many people we know who have supervised contract review can share stories of the missed provisions they have found in the course of this work (and, no doubt, many of those stories involve finding misses at inconvenient times; Noah remembers finding review problems late one Thursday evening with a report due to the client on Friday morning—it was a late night). In the case of due diligence contract review, results are sometimes further refined into high-level summaries, descriptive reports, and disclosure schedules. In many corporate use cases, results are imported into other software, like contract management systems. The (status quo) contract review process (i) is slow and costly, (ii) is prone to human error, and (iii) generates initial results that are not as useful as they might be with the assistance of technology.

AI Enhanced Contract Analysis

There are several reasons why the status quo, or manual review, does not measure up to AI-enhanced contract review. First of all, it's super time-consuming, since it takes the average person anywhere from one to five minutes a page to read a contract in order to find the important information, and a contract can be 5, 15, 50, or even more than 100 pages long. Contracts can be very complicated, and this is a lot of work.

Next, while the lawyers doing this work are very proficient, and often come to top law firms from the best law schools where they did very well, they can still screw it up. Why? There are two primary reasons: systematic and random errors. The *systematic* component of review errors is that the people who are doing the contract review work don't always know what they're looking for. Reviewers tend to be junior lawyers, and even though they may have gone to an excellent law school, such as Harvard or Columbia, law schools don't teach practical skills—like how to spot a change of control clause.

Ironically, the senior people who actually do know what to look for from their years of experience aren't the ones who are doing this work, at least in Biglaw. In small law, things work a little differently, with people at various levels doing a little bit of everything, so a senior attorney will likely be more involved in reviewing contracts.

There's also a cost factor that comes into play. A true story of a senior attorney at a major firm, Matt, who explained that he could do the contract review project in two hours and that it would take an associate two days. "But the client doesn't feel like paying me to do the project in two hours at $1,000 an hour, so junior lawyers do it instead in two days," explained Matt. Of course, this was not as cost-effective to the client. If it was going to take Matt two hours or cost $2,000 and an associate would charge $300 an hour but it would take roughly 16 hours, or $4,800, Matt was not saving the client money by having associates do the work.

The truth is, however, even if you had the top partners at Biglaw firms doing the reviews, it would still be problematic because they couldn't cover as much ground as AI. They're still human, and they would still have to read the contracts. While they would likely have a better idea of what to look for and where to find it, the stuff you're looking for is not always where it's supposed to be. For example, Noah once saw a change of control clause in a notice section, and that's not something you'd expect. It shouldn't have been there, but it was. Either way, a senior partner is still not faster than AI.

Then there's the *random* error component, which is simple; people at any size law firm are often doing this work for hours and hours. So, by the time it gets to 4:00 in the morning, for the second or third night in a row, they are no longer very sharp. There are also the distractions in life, such as having a fight with their girlfriend or boyfriend, or working with March Madness or the World Cup on TV in the background. Contract review is a high-focus task, and the glut of data to review makes it nearly impossible for even the sharpest humans to maintain a high level of concentration for long periods of time. Even after drinking several Red Bulls. The point is, people screw up.

Two Types of Contract Review

Contract analysis breaks down into two distinct types of contract review: pre-signature and post-signature. There are two situations at play with pre-signature contract review. First, you've got to create a contract. You can take a form and you can copy it or you can do something fancier, which might include AI to help you choose individual segments of an existing contract to create a new one.

Second, once you send your draft over to the other side and they see the contract, they're going to make comments. They may say this does or does not work for us because of *X, Y,* and *Z*. It might be that your payment terms are 90 days, but they need them to be 30 days, or the governing law is Sweden and they need it to be Delaware, or you say there's unlimited liability but in fact, they need liability to be capped at the value of the contract. That's what both sides do in the pre-signature review. They look at the terms and determine what is acceptable and what needs to be changed.

In post-signature review, you have a whole bunch of contracts that have already been signed. They're agreements that the company has approved, but now people need to pull data out of those contracts. Imagine you're a toy company with numerous contracts and you need to figure out what licenses you have and royalties you have to pay, or, because of COVID-19, you're trying to figure out which of the contracts have a force majeure clause in them and you need to see what that force majeure clause says because you're unable to ship toys because your outsourced manufacturers were closed. Can you get a delay, or are you required to deliver, despite the fact that the government has shut everything down?

The reality, when dealing with contracts, is that life happens. As a result, there's an ongoing need to refer back to contracts to determine what they say regarding numerous possible circumstances, the specific language, and how it can be interpreted to cover current or upcoming situations. Perhaps you're trying to do a merger and you need to find out what happens to the contracts in a change of control situation. This question likely has a concrete answer, so you need to go through the contracts to find and pull out that information. This takes time.

How AI-Based Contract Review Works

We've talked about the benefits of using AI over manual review; now let's talk about what the software itself actually does. When you do post-signature review over a figurative pile of contracts—75, several thousand, or even millions of them—you will likely be looking at relatively consistent information across those contracts. Maybe that means five data points, maybe a hundred or more.

The idea is simple. First, you load the contracts into the software (via drag and drop, or more automatically from another piece of software like a virtual data room). You then need to tell the software what you need it to find in the contracts, or, perhaps, the software takes a guess at what you're looking for automatically. Kira, for example, comes out of the box trained to find over 1,100 different things in contracts. However, you may only need it to find five, so you let Kira know which five data points to look for. The software has been taught to find these provisions. For example, it knows what a change of control clause looks like from looking at thousands of examples of them. The software reads through the contracts and finds text that looks like a change of control clause, pulls it out, and then allows users to review what the system has found. Note that the software is looking for concepts, not words. A clause needn't have the words *change of control* in it to get identified. These findings also go into summary charts, which can take a variety of forms, including organized lists of verbatim clauses, summarized provisions, and answers to questions. In the case of due diligence contract review, results are sometimes further refined into high-level summaries, descriptive reports, and disclosure schedules (see Figure 10.1).

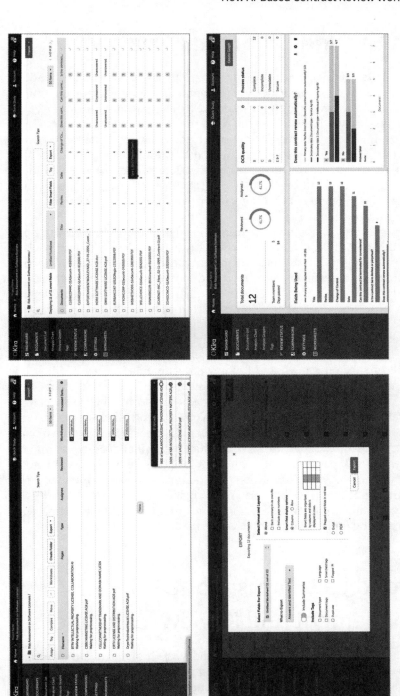

FIGURE 10.1   Contract analysis with Kira clockwise from top left (Importing, Viewing Results, Dashboard, Export Prep).

Familiar and Unfamiliar Contracts

When looking for a contract review system, it may be worth your while to consider whether the majority of your contracts are familiar or unfamiliar. Sometimes the contracts to be reviewed are simply executed versions of form agreements, and reviewers have the form in advance. Imagine a large technology company considering all of its executed system integrator agreements, an insurance company needing to extract data from its own policies, a landlord looking at leases it executed over a short time period in a given building, a bank needing to get through a pile of ISDAs, or someone trying to review a folder of NDAs completed on their own paper. All of these situations might feature "known documents."

Automatically extracting data from known documents is easy. Since provisions are known in advance, searchers can write rules or train models to closely fit the form. But diversity reigns in typical contract review. The form and wording of agreements to be reviewed in most contract reviews are typically not known in advance. This is especially true in M&A due diligence reviews of a target company's contracts, but is also regularly the case in contract management database population work—even the biggest companies negotiate their contracts, and regularly execute agreements on others' paper. These unknown-in-advance agreements are "unfamiliar documents."

Performance on known and unknown documents is a big dividing line in automated contract review software systems. If all you seek is data from known documents, pretty much any system should be able to meet your technical needs, and you can make a decision based on other user experience factors. If, however, you need to review unfamiliar documents, you will need a system that can accurately extract data from unfamiliar documents, and not every system will perform at the same level. This is where you will need to understand how a system performs on unfamiliar contracts, and how well it can be trained to find the nuances in unfamiliar documents. Whether the vast majority of your documents are familiar or unfamiliar will factor into what you are looking for in a contract review system.

Beyond Law Firms: Contract Management and Review in Business

Almost all mid- to large-size companies today are inundated with contracts. Growth exacerbates the problem. In an effort to better understand the relationships that those contracts represent, companies should set up a contract management database. A contract management database allows a company to know when their contracts expire, what renewal provisions are in them, what their indemnification or assignment rules are, and so much more. There are lots of options available for contract management databases, ranging from spreadsheets or homegrown Sharepoint-based implementations, up to dedicated software solutions (of which there are plenty of choices). Yet many companies don't have one.

Having a contract management database is only half the battle. A database is useless without data in it. Although many contract management systems offer drafting tools that will autopopulate the database for newly created documents, enterprises can have vast numbers of legacy contracts with information that won't be in the contract management database unless someone puts it there. That's where automated contract review software can help in a big way. Finding data from contracts to put into a contract management database takes real time. A contract review system can do this automatically, or help human reviewers do their work faster and more accurately. That's not all. Even when a company assiduously uses document-generation software that autopopulates data points to a contract management system, what matters to a company in its contracts can change over time, meaning its lawyers might need to find information they never thought to retain. Here, too, AI contract analysis software can help.

The bottom line is that companies should have good visibility into what their contracts say in aggregate, and they don't today. If and where implemented, these databases provide greater access to information across a business, which helps to mitigate risks and reveal opportunities. As companies grow, their number of contracts often increases rapidly. Since contracts define business relationships, it is important to know what is inside each of those contracts. That is where using AI for contract review and management can benefit any company.

THE ROI OF AI: HOW A LARGE FIRM DETERMINES IT

By Alicia Ryan, a Former Corporate Attorney and Now Senior Manager of Practice Innovation at a Leading Am Law 100 Firm

We brought in our first AI tool in 2016 to handle contract review. It was relatively early on in the scheme of legal tech emergence, but AI for contract analysis was not something that we were going to build in-house; it was something that made sense to purchase.

The target area for us was, and still is, M&A due diligence. It's an area that's ripe for innovation because it's rote work that attorneys don't love and it's time-intensive, so it can cause sticker-shock to clients, even in relatively non-price-sensitive M&A matters.

During the first year of implementation, we spent a lot of time trying to wrap our heads around exactly what the ROI would be. How could we measure it quantitatively and qualitatively? Could we explain what we were actually getting and make it clear to other attorneys, relationship partners, and clients? What was the value add? The answer to this turned out to be more nuanced than we expected.

On the quantitative side, we did a limited study of due diligence on deals pre-AI and then post-AI. To do this, I first talked to the review teams to identify 20 deals (10 pre-AI and 10 post-AI) that were comparable in both numbers of documents and level of review. I then reviewed individual time entries to determine which tasks would have been impacted by the use of the new AI tool and compared billings for those types of tasks across the two deal sets. What we found was that with the AI assist, the team was spending 20–60% less time on the same tasks that they had done manually prior to using AI. (The median time-savings was 50%.) Of course, contract review doesn't impact every task in due diligence, so this is not to say that clients' due diligence bills went down by 50%, but for every task that utilized AI in such a capacity, the median time saved was 50%.

We are also using contract review and analysis software in the knowledge management department to support the production of our publications and precedent databases—anything that requires a survey of deal terms. In this vein, we've trained the software to assist us in reviewing corporate charters, proxy statements, convertible promissory notes, and other documents of interest to attorneys or clients. It's the same work, it's just not for M&A.

Our most recent effort is to combine our AI tool with some additional programming to create an expert assistant for the review of certain types of agreements. We've started with NDAs for the prototype. The assistant tells the reviewer which provisions are present in the document and which provisions are missing, along with a red, yellow, or green indicator as well as suggested alternative language and annotations. The goal of this is to codify expert input and present it at the time of review so junior attorneys can do a more thorough and cost-effective first-pass review.

Training a contract analysis AI tool is a little bit art and a little bit science, but it doesn't require thousands (or even hundreds) of documents and shouldn't scare off potential users. The more similar the documents, and the more similar the terms, the fewer documents it takes to train the software. In agreements that are similar or have similar provisions, we've found that you can train using 20 documents and it takes just a few minutes.

Reviewing the Reviews

When implementing an AI system, managing expectations will be important. Attorneys always need to check (or at least spot-check) the review. Don't assume this is obvious. You will get users with expectations at both ends of the spectrum. Either they think it's never going to work and they never give it a chance, or they think it's AI and, therefore, it's going to be perfect, so they can just rely on it without checking. Neither of these is true, ever.

An AI reviewer is not a human reviewer—it's an algorithm, so on your transaction or your batch of documents, it's always going to get the same results. Either the same correct results or the same incorrect results. That's why you check. For example, if you check the first 10 out of 1,000 contracts, and it is correctly finding a specific clause, it will find that clause in the remaining 990. Conversely, if it misses a particular clause or variation of a clause because it's not something the AI was trained to look for, it will not catch it at any time. You will have 1,000 false negatives. But a spot check will show you the error, and you can then go back and train the system to search for this additional provision. But if you don't look, you won't know. So the system only works well when AI and humans work together.

How Contract Analysis Software Is Impacting How Lawyers Work

Contract analysis AI is proving to have several positive impacts on legal practice. Three areas most positively affected are: the kind of work junior lawyers can do; the law firm's ability to make more money; and the overall quality of the lawyer's work product.

Entry-level lawyers should not be upset with the increased use of AI-assisted contract review. While we sympathize with law graduates having a hard time finding employment, we believe AI will create more new legal work than it will destroy (as described in Chapter 2). Further, the work that AI takes away from junior lawyers is not work they would enjoy doing if they had to do it. In fact, when Noah was a first-year lawyer at a large NYC law firm, some of the work was challenging and interesting, but a decent portion of it felt like it could have been done by someone making far less money, who might still have done an excellent job. At first you're happy to take on such tedious work, knowing that you're being well compensated. But it doesn't take long before you feel very unfulfilled and disenchanted with your new legal career.

Using contract review AI provides junior lawyers with an opportunity to do more interesting, more challenging work. Interesting, challenging work typically makes junior lawyers happier in their jobs and more likely to stay at their firms longer.

Technology can also help law firms make more money, as described in Chapter 2. Contract analysis AI can increase the quality of lawyer work product.

Specially designed software systems focused on improving a specific legal process can lead to findings that a human might miss. This is especially true when the lawyer being supplemented is recently out of law school, unfamiliar with the task in question, tired, and not enthusiastic about that part of the project.

Good lawyers and firms add significant value to the transactions on which they are involved. For this they are, and will continue to be, well compensated. There may be changes in the legal industry, but providers of quality legal services who embrace change and deliver value should continue to be successful.

In its 2019 Technology Survey, the International Legal Technology Association (ILTA) asked its members which machine-learning–based tools their organizations used. Of the top seven solutions named by respondents, four of them are in the contract analysis space (in order of responses): Kira, RAVN/iManage, Luminance, and eBrevia. The footprint of these contract analysis companies continues to expand; Kira counts 60% of the top 50 Am Law 200 firms, including 7 of the U.S. "Vault 10," 11 of the top 12 UK firms measured by revenue, and 5 of the "Seven Sisters" Canadian firms among its customers. Luminance claims to have over 250 customers across the world, including one-fifth of the Global 100 law firms.

TIGHT DEADLINE

By Amy Monaghan, Senior Practice Innovations Manager at Perkins Coie LLP

Our attorneys were working quickly for a client in the middle of a fast-tracked M&A transaction. The client had a small budget and a tight deadline (signatures were due five days from the day the partner received the phone call). Initially, the client planned to handle the acquisition internally without engaging outside counsel but ran into some issues where they needed assistance. We quickly spun together a project team that consisted of the partner, Knowledge Management, and the leads for our contract review service to iron out scope and deliverables.

We had just started our pilot with Kira but I had used Kira before at my previous law firm and I knew what it could do for custom model training on non-M&A matters. This time, however, we would need to put it to the test on the M&A work. Would it work? With this kind of deadline, we sure hoped so.

We worked out a plan with the client to run a test batch of documents through to gauge Kira's utility for this particular review project and developed a pricing model and project plan based on the results. The client initially wanted a high-priority red flag review because both time and budget were limited.

So, we ran the test batch through Kira and closely analyzed the results. We determined that Kira would work well on the deal so we proceeded with the plan. In the end, we were able to produce a more comprehensive report than the client had expected, thanks to the assistance of the technology. Plus, we met the tight deadline *and* stayed within budget! In fact, we even made a small profit. The most important outcome was that we were able to provide services that exceeded expectations, both for our partner and for our client.

The Future of AI and Contract Analysis

We see AI driving three big changes in the contract analysis space:

1. *An increase in the size and scope of contract review for law firms and enterprises.* Historically, instead of reviewing all possibly relevant contracts—whether 5,000 or 500,000—reviews would be limited to a sample because it had to be done by manual review. Reviewing the total population simply wasn't practical. Now, with contract analysis software, law firms no longer have to be limited by the number of people available to put on a project. Enterprises won't avoid making a decision because they don't know what is included in the details of specific contracts. The expectation will be formed in the enterprise that they have ubiquitous access to information. This is similar to what we covered in Chapter 7. Before the advent of eDiscovery tools, it simply wasn't possible to conduct these massive reviews. In the case of eDiscovery, technology caused an explosion of data sources, which led to enormous reviews, which in turn led to technology innovation to effectively conduct these reviews. In the case of contract analysis, AI will drive lawyers to do analysis the way it should be done because now they can.

   The tools themselves will need to change to help lawyers manage these larger reviews and the volumes of data. They'll need to be more focused and granular, directing users to where they should look. AI will serve as an essential collaborator on contract reviews.

2. *We will see more AI contract applications.* We are seeing drafting and negotiation tools with embedded playbooks, but no doubt we will start to see other, more interesting tools that we can't even imagine. Tools that predict what outcomes would look like if you took one position or another, or quickly added up all your risks on a contract. Tools that enable greater interaction between lawyers and contracts. Accurate data extraction is a necessary foundation for building many exciting contract intelligence applications.

3. *We anticipate more competitors and ideas coming into this space.* When we started Kira, there were only three or four companies in the space, and now there are heaps. An influx of VC funding has been coming into contract analysis. Remember the MarTech 5000 landscape summary from Chapter 4? We fully anticipate that Contract Analysis will form its own well-populated category over the next few years, much like many of the big sub-categories of the Marketing Tech space.

CHAPTER 11

Expert Systems

Self-Service Law and the Automation of Legal Question-Answering

By Michael Mills

Co-Founder and Chief Strategy Officer of Neota Logic

A I in law, across all its many forms, is fundamentally about one intellectual process—inference: if A, then B. Laws and regulations are written as inferences. Law schools train lawyers in legal inference. In practice, lawyers make inferences all day. That's what, in a sense, clients engage lawyers to do. They build if-then statements in their minds. If there is some fact or pattern of facts that we can observe with some degree of accuracy and certainty, then we can conclude some other things.

We can say: "If X, Y, and Z happen, then you have this risk." We can say: "If this paragraph includes this cloud of words in these relationships, then it is probably a governing law clause." We can say: "This patent law claim in the Northern District of California will likely be decided for the claimant on motion." We can construct sets of inferences about domains of knowledge, from tax law to derivatives contracts.

In each case, we also say, or at least try to say, that our inference is made with some realistically estimated degree of confidence. Seat-of-the-pants judgments, the compressed compilations of experience that some call "expertise" or "intuition," are of course valid and useful. But that's not how AI does inference. It is important that we understand degree of confidence. It is also important to the accuracy, credibility, and defensibility of our inferences that we explain our reasoning with some degree of clarity. What data did we consider? What methods did we apply?

Expert systems are one form of AI in law, using symbolic logic to represent facts and inferences in explicit, traceable structures that map directly to the structures of statutes and regulations, and the structures that human experts use when explaining their reasoning. This short answer to the question "What are expert systems?" will be expanded throughout this chapter.

Some Background: Founding Neota Logic

I am a lawyer. I graduated from the University of Chicago Law School, clerked for a federal judge, worked in a big law firm in New York City, became a partner in another big law firm, mostly doing litigation and bankruptcy. I was then recruited by Davis Polk in a newly created role, which today might be called chief innovation officer. My charter was the *how* of law practice—marshaling processes, technologies, and professionals other than lawyers to optimize service to clients.

I always remember sitting in my first-year law school evidence class thinking I could write a program that embodies the rules of evidence. I didn't get around to doing it while I was in law school, but I was convinced that it could be done. For a while, I did a lot of tax work and recognized how a computer, if properly coded, could answer significant tax questions. TurboTax is proof of that. Indeed, TurboTax is the largest and most widely used expert system in the law—encoding the personal tax parts of the federal Internal Revenue Code and 50 state tax codes.

While I was working at Davis Polk, the firm had been commissioned to do a multi-jurisdictional study in a complex and evolving area of international derivatives law. The firm retained lawyers all around the world. Working together, they brilliantly analyzed, normalized, and packaged the results of the long and complex study in enough black binders to fill a long bookshelf. When the clients took a look at the binders, they said: "Thank you. This is impressive, and certainly worth the large amount we paid you for it. But in fact, what we really want is not the research; that's just the foundation. We want answers. We have business people who are trying to make a decision about a particular transaction."

High-speed, high-dollar transactions needed answers quickly, not a five-foot-long shelf of black binders. It was at that time that I decided to turn to expert systems technology to build a solution that answered the client's questions. That system has been updated regularly and is still in use by one of the largest banks in the country.

After leaving Davis Polk, I co-founded Neota Logic in 2010 with two other lawyers, long-time friends of mine and entrepreneurs who, like me, had decided that creating technology for law practice was more fun than practicing law itself. At that time, with the "great recession" still going, clients were more attuned than ever to cost-efficiency. Law firms were opening their minds to innovation. We knew that expert systems could improve legal services, not only for corporate clients and their firms but also for consumer, pro bono, and legal aid clients.

What Sets Expert Systems Apart?

In AI in the law field, there are five principal avenues to value:

1. Legal research
2. Electronic discovery
3. Contract analysis—pre-signature and post-signature
4. Predictive analytics—court processes and outcomes; pricing and legal operations; government processes
5. Expertise automation

Expertise automation is my field. We use inference techniques to automate expertise about the three things lawyers know and do—substantive law, documents, and processes. When we started the business, there were only two of us in the field. The other was Oracle Intelligent Advisor (formerly Policy Automation), which is used by the Internal Revenue Service and many other government agencies. Lately, we have been joined by half a dozen startups.

What distinguishes expert systems from machine learning tools? The answer is threefold: (i) how facts and patterns are observed; (ii) how inferential statements are constructed; and (iii) how results are explained.

For expert systems, facts and patterns are observed, and inferences are constructed, by human experts, sometimes with the assistance of knowledge engineers who understand both the topic domain and the technology. Experts map the topic explicitly, building rules that can be instantiated in software. Modern expert systems tools make rule-building easy, like drawing on a whiteboard, so experts can work quickly and efficiently and immediately test what they have done. Results are deterministic and explainable: rules can be traced with 100% transparency, and produce precise repeatable results.

For machine learning systems, we start with data, as much as we can gather—examples of documents, records of decisions, or transactions. We then begin the iterative process: apply human-selected algorithms to attempt inferences, test results, select different algorithms and/or tune algorithms, measure the confidence factor, test, tune, test . . . and so on. This is usually called *learning* and there are three principal types (increasingly with many subtle variants): *unsupervised* (let the algorithms do the best they can); *supervised* (have humans "train" the algorithm or confirm its results, as was done for the massive image classifiers at Google and other companies); and *reinforcement* (create a feedback loop between an outcome and the algorithm, as was done by DeepMind to train game-playing systems). In law, we almost always use supervised learning, with some unsupervised (or clustering) to seed the supervised process.

Dr. Andrew Ng, one of the world's leading experts on AI, explained a few years ago in a *Harvard Business Review* article that machine learning techniques are fundamentally good at classification.[1] I've got a pile of things. I can look at them and I can put them in smaller piles. In electronic discovery, I can say, "This is about issue X, or issue Y, it's relevant or not, privileged or not." In contract analysis, I can say, "It's this kind of clause. And it is consistent with or inconsistent with the model that I have in mind." Expert systems can deal with much more fine-grained outcomes, such as the exact steps to follow to comply with data breach laws in the State of Virginia.

Machine learning tools measure their degree of confidence statistically. Feedback cycles aim to produce higher and higher degrees of confidence. There's a lot of work being done toward "explainable AI"—it even has an acronym, XAI—trying to reverse engineer or give a backward-looking view into the algorithms that machine learning systems generate. Nevertheless, outcomes are irreducibly probabilistic. You get a confidence factor of $X\%$ and make a judgment whether that is sufficient in the context—topic domain, problem type, frequency, cost, time, downside risk of wrong outcomes, regulatory requirements, and so on.

Expert system rules are created by humans. These rules are explicit and deterministic rather than statistical and probabilistic, so the outcome confidence factor is 100%. (Correctness is a different concept: bad experts can create bad rules that generate bad results with 100% confidence. The analogy in machine learning is wrong outcomes, or biased outcomes, based on poorly selected or biased data.) The tradeoff for expert systems' transparency and certainty is that human knowledge engineering is not free, and not infinite. Building good rules across a large domain is hard work. We, therefore, build systems to answer questions in domains of reasonable scope and stability. Although less human input may be required, machine learning systems must also be carefully focused on specific problems (no artificial general intelligence chatter in law, please).

Expert systems in law deliver self-help—efficient, scalable answers to relatively routine legal questions at high volume and low cost. Can I do this? What are the risks if I do that? What are the procedures I need to follow in order to do X, Y, or Z? In a cost-conscious world, being able to answer those relatively routine questions in an automated way is a compelling story to government agencies, corporate legal departments, and law firms, as well as other legal service providers.

ComplianceHR is a joint venture between Neota Logic and the law firm Littler Mendelson. ComplianceHR does not sell technology; it sells complete expert systems that answer employment law questions, combining Littler's legal expertise with Neota Logic's technology.

If, for example, a supervisor in the Phoenix branch of a big company is uncertain whether an employee should be paid overtime, they *might* find a handbook written last year by a lawyer in the home office in Connecticut. The handbook might be current. And the supervisor might find the right section in the book and might apply the principles correctly. Certainly, the company won't allow calling outside counsel: too expensive for routine matters. And the in-house counsel in Connecticut is busy writing the new handbook.

A better solution is a quick check with an interactive expert system. It asks a few questions about the employee and the context and then delivers an actionable answer. Or, in a tricky case, the system will send an email with all the facts to the lawyer in Connecticut for decision.

Although the question is from one perspective "routine," the right answer has business value. If the company makes an occasional wrong decision about overtime, a few employees are annoyed. But if the answer is wrong repeatedly, the company risks an enforcement action or a complaint for discriminatory application of overtime rules. Expert systems provide defensible answers, reduced compliance costs, reduced litigation risks, improved employee morale (because they get prompt answers), and more productive time for in-house lawyers.

Another example: data privacy. A bank in London receives a subpoena from a court in New York City for documents about employees and transactions in Frankfurt. Does it need to comply? How? A corporation in Vermont is the victim of a data breach involving customers in six states. Who must be notified? What form of notice to whom? Must the customers be compensated? Every state's rules are different. An expert system can provide immediate, state-specific, fact-specific, customer-specific answers.

Who's Using Expert Systems? And Why?

We find four main categories of expert system users: law firms, corporate legal departments, and legal publishers, as well as the consultants who assist them.

Law firms build expert systems for internal efficiency or quality assurance and, more often, for service to clients. In so many practices, differentiation between firms is difficult. One answer is to productize a practice group's expertise on a specific topic. Enabling clients to obtain low-cost solutions to routine problems creates "sticky" relationships that lead to full-service engagements when the problems are no longer routine. Our law firm customers often initiate building an expert system because they have a specific problem for a specific client or practice. Then they discover that the technology is adaptable to many different problems and practices, and it is easy to use.

Corporate legal departments have been and continue to be under intense pressure from company management to reduce legal spend. The traditional methods are to do more work in-house (hiring more lawyers to do it) and extract discounts from law firms. Over the last decade, the toolbox has expanded to include "law companies" (alternative legal service providers) and technology. One key technology is expert systems, which enable in-house lawyers to offload the routine work and concentrate on the important work, the top-of-license work that calls for imagination and judgment. (As one general counsel said to the deputy GC for employment law, "Stop doing stupid stuff.")

How does a legal department provide self-help drafting of nondisclosure agreements to its internal clients? Surely that's simple. Not exactly—when there are 20 business units in 30 countries, 15 master forms for different business relationships in three languages, and three legal teams. The rules get *quite* complex, beyond the capability of document automation systems but easy for a true expert system inference engine. Also complex are the workflows for business and legal approval, counterparty negotiation, electronic signature, and document retention, all integrated with HR and other internal systems.

Legal publishers use expert systems to supplement traditional research materials. Thomson Reuters Tax & Accounting, for example, has embedded more than 100 Neota Logic expert systems in the TR Checkpoint Tax Service, which is used by thousands of tax professionals. To solve a tax problem with Checkpoint, start by searching or browsing to the statutes and regulations, then read the cited cases and expert commentary by TR editors, then run an expert system to apply the rules to specific fact patterns and test alternative solutions.

Avocado Toast

Machine learning algorithms, predictive analytics algorithms, symbolic logic—all have a place in the law and are often most powerful when combined.

An example of algorithms and logic in action together comes from Allens, one of the leading law firms in Australia. In the firm's real estate practice, lawyers need to evaluate the legal effects and risks in portfolios of leases when office buildings, shopping centers, and other large properties are bought, sold, and financed. The work is constant, fast-paced, and cost-conscious.

The Allens' innovation team first formed an interdisciplinary team for lease review, allocating the work to a mix of lawyers and others, then engaged Neota Logic to build an expert system to guide the review with a logic-driven questionnaire to assure that the necessary deep detail was collected when needed, but only then. From a pool of several hundred potential questions, the system—which Allens named REDDA, Real Estate Due Diligence App—asks, for any individual lease, only the few dozen questions that are needed for the specific property type and commercial terms. As the partner in charge described it, REDDA "embeds more than 20 years of legal knowledge into a tool that analyses leases and flags material issues that require further review." After the review is complete, REDDA evaluates the risk of each lease and the full portfolio and prepares a report for Allens' client. With the Neota Logic application, the review team's productivity increased by 30%, and client costs were reduced by 30%.

Allens then orchestrated a collaboration between Neota Logic and Kira Systems to improve productivity and quality even more. REDDA now takes advantage of the strengths of both platforms. Kira "reads" the leases, classifies them, identifies and extracts key clauses, and extracts some structured data such as party names and dates. Primed with the Kira output, the Neota Logic expert system guides lawyers through their review, which focuses on the deep details that machine learning cannot parse, such as interrelationships among provisions, consistency, and ambiguity. Again, when review is complete, the system does an evaluation and report.

As for the term "Avocado Toast," in 2017, Noah Waisberg of Kira Systems and Richard Seabrook of Neota Logic won the prize for best props at Legal Geek, a vibrant London-based Legal Tech community conference, for their presentation on the Neota Logic and Kira Systems collaboration when they literally brought a toaster, an avocado, and a loaf of bread on stage to construct a metaphor of bricolage—the bringing together of diverse things to create something new. Just as avocado and toast coming together have led to a trendy growth in avocado toast sales, the combination of technologies also represents the future of AI in the law. As Noah noted in a packed talk at the International Legal Technology Association's annual conference (ILTACON), it is said in *Lord of the Rings* that there is no one magic ring that does everything. Indeed, Neota Logic is designed to enable customers to use "any algorithm you need." The hybrid reasoning engine combines symbolic logic with other algorithms from any system—contract analysis from Kira, Excel spreadsheets from Microsoft, complex mathematics from Wolfram, predictive analytics from BigML, and so on.

Looking Ahead

Along with algorithmic avocado toast, the future of AI in law is simplicity and user experience. Algorithms are available off-the-shelf from specialists like Kira and generalists like Amazon, Facebook, Google, IBM, Microsoft, and

Wolfram (in alphabetical order), and are increasingly packaged so that they can be used by non-specialists. At Neota Logic, we have made it easy to plug those algorithms into hybrid expert systems.

From the beginning, our goal has been a no-code, no-programmer tool that can be learned quickly and used easily. We have trained more than a thousand law students, lawyers, and other professionals to use our tools. Of course, "easy to use" is rather like the holy grail, always to be pursued but never quite reached, so we aim in every iteration to improve user experience. We believe that expert systems and other AI tools for law, as they become easier to use, will become ubiquitous among lawyers, like Excel among financial analysts.

In the real world of people delivering services, process is everything. Legal answers and artifacts are part of a larger process—some set of actions toward a personal or business goal. Law itself is a process—multiple tasks done by multiple people over time, planned, assisted, and managed intelligently. Thus, the future of AI in law reaches beyond hybrid reasoning and integration of algorithms to the orchestration of complex flows of work by people and systems.

Note

1. Ng, Andrew. 2016. What artificial intelligence can and cannot do right now. *Harvard Business Review* (November 9). https://hbr.org/2016/11/what-artificial-intelligence-can-and-cant-do-right-now

PART III

The Plan

Leverage data and AI to expand
and future proof your practice

CHAPTER 12

The AI Adoption Framework

Understanding the Adoption Path That Will Help You Get Ahead and Build the Practice of the Future

There are numerous ways that AI can enhance the delivery of legal services. AI is central to modern technology assisted review (TAR) in litigation; in legal research; in contract analysis; in expert systems; and in litigation analytics. In all of these applications, AI systems benefit lawyers by streamlining many of the more mundane tasks within legal workflows, while also helping them locate the best answers and make better legal decisions. In short, AI can help. It is already helping many law firms and in-house legal departments practice law more efficiently and make data-supported decisions.

But how does a legal organization determine whether it is fully leveraging AI's benefits? The maturity of an organization's use of AI can be seen as the interplay between two factors: (i) the extent to which it has adopted AI in its work, and (ii) the "creativity" with which it's using AI. The former is mostly about how widespread AI use is in appropriate contexts; the latter is more about the skill and flexibility with which the AI is deployed.

Factor 1: Comprehensive Use of AI

The first factor to consider is the extent to which an organization is using AI in every situation in which it can have significant impact, considering the firm's mix of legal services. For example, a law firm that focuses on litigation will likely leverage AI in its eDiscovery practice, using TAR wherever it can.

Via TAR, AI will be used to review large sets of electronic documents in an effort to identify documents that are responsive to a discovery request. The firm might also use AI-enhanced legal research software to find the most relevant cases; litigation analysis tools to review the case history of opposing counsel and recent decisions made by the judge serving on the case; and an AI-based brief checking tool to analyze the firm's or an opposing party's court briefs.

A firm that does limited litigation but has a large transactional practice might adopt entirely different forms of AI, such as contract analysis software, in order to perform document reviews, or expert systems to help lawyers answer recurring questions around complicated securities or tax regulations.

An in-house law department might use TAR software to help it respond to litigation discovery requests (perhaps through a law firm, perhaps through another eDiscovery service provider, perhaps through using their internal people), and also to proactively avoid litigation risk through information governance. They might answer employment or trading questions with the help of customized expert systems. And they might deploy contract analysis AI to help better understand and leverage their contract estate, as well as an AI contract negotiation tool to turn agreements faster.

A law firm or an in-house legal department might also adopt AI in its business operations. Many organizations now use time and billing software that can, for example, use matter data to monitor performance, establish pricing and budgets, and determine how to appropriately resource matters.

The level of AI adoption will clearly differ based on the size of the organization, type of law being practiced, number and type of clients, and even the organization's culture and level of risk aversion.

All things being equal, a firm with a default strategy to use AI-based contract analysis on every due diligence review process is clearly more deeply engaged with AI than a firm that uses AI on only 10% of its deals. Similarly, an in-house legal department that is applying AI to analyze outside counsel spend, to plan budgets and set pricing, and to measure lawyer productivity or practice area profitability is clearly more engaged with AI than a department that has acquired a single AI-based product as a point solution to a single business problem.

Widespread adoption of technologies, including AI, are driven by a complex set of attitudes, practices, behaviors, and mindsets. Those drivers include:

- An established technology evaluation and acquisition process.
- Staff with legal operations skills, who can deploy AI solutions with an understanding of the underlying legal processes they support.
- Strong data management and governance practices, which ensure that the data used by AI systems is accurate and authoritative.
- Policies that allow (or encourage) use of new tools.
- A focus on user experience, including strong integration of new tools with existing workflows.

- Strong training and communications processes, including the sharing of successes across practice area boundaries.
- Support from senior leadership.
- Client pressure (or support).
- Enthusiastic end users.

Factor 2: The Breadth and Creativity of AI Use

The second factor is how creative the organization is when it comes to using AI, including the breadth of different applications it finds for AI. For some organizations, the use of "off the rack" AI systems will suffice. But as they become familiar with the technology, some organizations become more adept at customizing AI in ways that augment and amplify their own expertise. This includes, for example, creating their own AI models to identify and extract language from texts that are specific to their own practice rather than using models that come with the software "out of the box." Users of Kira's Quick Study capability are showing this kind of creativity in their use of AI; they see opportunities to leverage contract review capabilities beyond the standard offering.

Other organizations show creativity by training AI systems to expand the organization's advantages, or capabilities, in certain areas of law, or custom integrating various pieces of technology together. This can involve doing a review, or taking inventory of the firm's necessary tasks and determining which ones could benefit from the use of AI:

- A firm with a large transactional practice might use AI tools to mine past deals as an exercise in knowledge management. Machine-learning analysis of past deals establishes deal points to help guide future transactions, but can also create an effective database of expertise, making it easy to identify experts in certain kinds of deals.
- A firm with a large regulatory practice might spend a lot of time with clients answering routine questions about the application of regulatory regimes to their day-to-day business practices. That firm might benefit from creating rules-based expert systems that allow clients a certain level of self-service for those kinds of questions. That firm is leveraging AI by embodying expertise in an automated system that can deliver client service 24/7, without "live" human interaction.

In these examples, AI is applied in a way that amplifies and extends key competitive advantages that come from the firm's specialized practice areas.

Another measure of creativity is the extent to which the output from the use of AI is integrated with other systems and workflows in the organization. For example, a corporation might use AI to extract terms and clauses from a large set of contracts to organize and store them in a contract management system. Some of those contract terms might be relevant to other business processes outside the legal department. Data about expiration dates in the contracts, for example, can be useful for business planning purposes. Other data might identify patterns that benefit finance, HR, marketing, or production. While some legal AI tools integrate with other pieces of technology, there are still many pieces of software that don't come with built-in integrations. The company can use application programming interfaces (APIs) to connect that expiration date data with other business planning software to create alerts about upcoming possible expirations.

Weightmans LLP is a good example of a law firm applying AI creatively. Among other strengths, Weightmans has a Chambers and Partners "Band 1" personal injury defense practice. They took Kira (which tends to be primarily used to review contracts and related documents) and trained it themselves on personal injury court forms and medical reports to find (among other things) accident details, evidence of hearing protection provision, or a medical prognosis. They then integrated it with MatterSphere (their matter management workflow software) using Kira's API. They went further and worked with the University of Liverpool's Computer Science Department to make use of recent AI developments, particularly from the field of computational argumentation, to model legal reasoning and challenges within this such as reflecting changes in the law.

This recent academic research was utilized to capture legal knowledge across different domains, including noise-induced hearing loss and slips and trips claims, which was then put into the Neota Logic expert system to make decision support tools to assist lawyers in reaching a liability decision. The combination of these technologies and approach improves the quality, consistency, and speed of decision-making, allowing lawyers to make good tactical decisions for clients. It also ensures that lawyers are freed up to work on cases where they can add the most value and impact for clients.

Dr. Catriona Wolfenden, Partner and Innovation Manager, commented:

> We saw the massive potential in Kira from the start and were keen to put it to use in less traditional areas, quickly appreciating that we could move away from single point solutions to create joined up tech ecosystems, allowing us to offer new and innovative services to clients. Projects such as this have been pivotal in changing conversations with clients, moving away from strictly legal discussions to a much wider dialogue about collaborative problem solving and digital transformation, in turn leading to the commencement of other innovative projects.

Another area where AI can help legal organizations is in building intelligence and automation into pricing and budgeting. Companies such as Digitory Legal help law firms and in-house legal departments automate the mining of billing and timekeeping data in order to predict and scope costs and budgets, resourcing requirements, and so on. Digitory uses AI-based predictive cost models to be able to make budgeting and pricing decisions, and track them. When that data is integrated into case management and firm/client collaboration platforms, those data and predictions become the basis for better decisions during the course of a matter; the creativity lies in extending the application of data generated through AI into multiple forms of decision-making.

How Mature Is Your Approach to AI?

The relationship between those two measures of an organization's approach to technology—the comprehensiveness of the use of AI and the creativity shown in applying it—says a lot about how well they are adapting to today's new way of practicing law. Their adoption maturity within a legal firm or corporate legal department can be plotted on a 2 × 2 grid using those two factors as the vertical and horizontal axes, as shown in Figure 12.1.

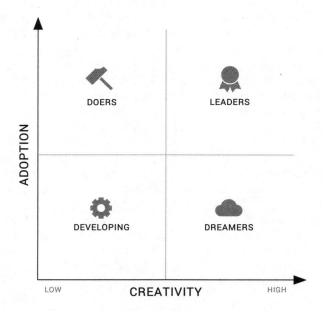

FIGURE 12.1   The AI maturity framework.

You can see that all organizations exist within one of the four quadrants in the grid. Let's examine each of those quadrants a little more closely.

Leaders 🎖

Show Strength in Adoption and Creativity—Now Need to Stay Focused to Stay on Top

A law firm in the Leaders quadrant will likely be using AI across practice areas where it maintains a competitive level of expertise. AI leveraged in TAR, in contract analysis, in expert systems will reach the level of "standard operating procedure," in the sense that the firm will start to see leveraging AI as something that is expected from all lawyers across all the firm's strategic practice areas. In addition, Leader firms will be those that fully leverage APIs and other tools that integrate the outputs from AI systems in workflow systems—significantly multiplying the impact of the AI by automating the appearance of data, predictions, and decision support into the tools that lawyers use on a day-to-day basis.

An in-house legal department that's in the Leaders quadrant is likely to be extending the business value it provides to its wider organization. Leaders include those who are adept at extracting data from the corporation's contracts or other data sources for purposes of planning, strategy, and various forms of business intelligence. For example, AI can be used to extract data on contract value, termination dates, lease terms, and so on. That data can then be automatically delivered to the company's various business intelligence softwares (e.g., ERP, CRM, HRIS). This company would fall into the Leaders quadrant—it is fully exploiting advanced features and achieving widespread adoption of AI.

Teams in this quadrant are doing well, but this is not a field in which complacency will likely be a successful strategy. To maintain their position, Leaders should focus on staying on top of AI developments, continuing to experiment and measure results, and constantly be searching for new opportunities to leverage AI.

Doers

Have Cleared a Big Adoption Hurdle— Now Can Extend by Expanding Their AI Expertise in New Ways

Where adoption is high across a variety of AI applications, but creativity in how AI is applied is less strong, a firm or in-house legal department falls into the Doers category. They are executing well to take advantage of AI tools they have, but might be leaving opportunity on the table. Achieving widespread adoption of any technology is a significant challenge. Being solidly positioned in the Doer category is a real accomplishment, and it may be enough for many organizations.

To move into the Leaders quadrant, this firm should consider focusing on practice areas and matters where the firm has deep expertise. Using the custom training features of AI software in projects will demonstrate to clients how that knowledge is magnified when embedded in AI-driven analysis of a document set. Another example of being more creative might come from a firm that does a high level of litigation between financial advisors and dissatisfied clients. Such a firm could use litigation analysis tools daily to size up the opposing counsel and/or the judge in upcoming cases. They could also demonstrate creativity by using expert systems to answer questions on recently updated SEC rule changes that affect how financial advisors are allowed to work with clients.

In short, moving from the Doers to the Leaders quadrant will require a more strategic approach to the application of AI in the organization. Rather than simply looking for efficiencies and cost savings, a big part of their challenge will be in looking to AI technology to provide them with differentiating advantages in critical service areas.

Dreamers

Show Some Big Ideas in the Organization—But Now Need to Beef Up Adoption

If creativity is high but adoption is low, the organization is missing out on the chance to fully benefit from AI. Those organizations can be seen as Dreamers. They may have identified proactive and creative ways to leverage AI, but they haven't been able to get their people to consistently apply best practice.

This category includes organizations with one or two enthusiasts digging deep into AI in their own domains or in clandestine skunk works, but where the rest of the organization lacks the same level of interest. Other organizations in this category engage in what we call "AI theater" or "innovation theater." Their efforts around AI and other technologies are largely marketing efforts directed more at garnering awards and press mentions than a deeper commitment to improving performance and client success. As an example, a transactions-oriented law firm might have an IP specialist using contract analysis tools in M&A due diligence reviews. That same individual may also have the skills to create and utilize models that illustrate her specific domain expertise in IP law. Other lawyers in the same firm, however, may not even be using AI on any of their deals, or even be aware that their colleague is an active user. Such a Dreamer firm is using AI in one-off, creative applications, but is missing out on the benefit of AI in more standard parts of firm practice.

Or the innovation or knowledge management team at a law firm might have expended lots of effort training an AI tool to work in a practice area they are strong in, and gone a step further by stitching together a number of pieces of software, delivering an excellent client experience. Their solution might be so compelling that it received positive press coverage and won multiple prestigious awards. It gets trotted out in new business pitches, and prospective clients love the sound of it. The only problem is that most lawyers in the firm still work the traditional pre-AI way, and the tool sits on the virtual shelf, gathering figurative dust. The firm feels good about its ability to execute on AI, but it shouldn't. In fact, this custom-build effort has arguably weakened the firm's AI capability. While, on the one hand, they conceived of something innovative and got it built, the partners of the firm know the truth: this innovation is a joke. The next time they hear about AI innovation, they may roll their eyes and snigger. They would be right to. This will make it harder for the firm to ever become a Doer. Implementation is key to successful AI adoption.

To move into the Leaders quadrant, Dreamer firms could increase, through training and/or incentives, a wider adoption of AI in the firm. The firm could also respond by changing staffing practices—for example, by identifying additional "power users" who can specialize in applying AI tools to contract reviews, in a consultative role supporting lawyers leading on deals. Good AI vendors may be able to suggest best practices they've seen work elsewhere. Getting senior leadership onboard (and vocal about their views) makes a big difference in adoption. Having clients provide positive (and negative) reinforcement can really help, too. Culture and leadership go a long way in driving organizations into the Leaders quadrant.

Developing ⚙

Lagging in Adoption and Creativity— Need to Focus First on Adoption to Gain Momentum

Finally, organizations that have neither adopted AI on a large-scale basis nor use it in any advanced or creative ways fall into the "Developing" category. This category also includes organizations that have licensed an AI-based product, but fail to grow adoption beyond a few users, or—worse yet—leave the product on the shelf. Firms in this category need to focus on identifying potential areas for AI, and then execute on a plan to implement it.

Organizations in this category may have managed to tread water and stay afloat despite outdated methods. They may recognize technological development as a necessary component of future growth, but they may lack the required leadership, skills, and strategic focus to really get off the ground. More likely, they are skeptical that they need to change what's worked for them in the past, and aren't convinced that being more efficient is in their economic best interests. Those that have yet to develop a plan of action regarding technology, or are just getting started, fall into the Developing category.

Organizations in the Developing quadrant can best begin their AI adoption journey by focusing on specific problems that they—and, more importantly, their clients—face in the way matters are currently addressed.

They can start by identifying work where accuracy is important, where the scale of the work makes human-based processes difficult, where work involves large volumes of data, where most of the work is simply repetitive and manual, and where well-compensated individuals are doing work that is below their true skill level. All of these are signs of work that could benefit from the application of AI.

Taking the Next Step

In the end, all law firms, legal departments, and solo law practitioners can benefit from the answering the following questions:

- Where are you today regarding technology and AI?
- What areas in your organization are not functioning up to their fullest?
- Where could AI help you extend your advantages?
- Have you reviewed technology designed for greater efficiency in these areas?
- What's holding you back, and how can you address these roadblocks?

To answer some more questions in order to help you fully adopt technology, go to AIForLawyersBook.com. Together, let's continue on this journey toward realizing the potential of AI for your practice and career.

CHAPTER 13

Conclusion

If you're ever in Stuttgart, Germany, the Mercedes-Benz Museum is well worth a visit. The museum is set up somewhat like the Guggenheim Museum in New York City, in which you start up at the top and then walk down a slowly spiraling ramp that takes you through exhibits that tell the story of this iconic car manufacturing company and—more interestingly—give a tangible tour through 135 years of technological advancement.

A high-quality scale model of a horse greets you when you get off the elevator at the top. It is there as a reminder that this was the most popular mode of personal transportation when the story begins. The first room after that features early products by founders Gottlieb Daimler and Carl Benz (who actually never met each other; the companies they started were merged in 1926). Benz's early vehicles (which are described as including the first "automobile," in 1886) look somewhat like a large tricycle with a motor on the back, with more of a joystick than a steering wheel (see Figure 13.1).

FIGURE 13.1 The Benz Patent-Motorwagen ("patent motorcar"), built in 1885, is widely regarded as the world's first production automobile.

Source: From Wikimedia Commons

Daimler's contemporaneous creations range from—essentially—a motorized bicycle to things that look like horse carts, with an engine instead of a horse.

Continuing down the spiraling path, you get to Daimler's 1901 Mercedes 35 HP (named after Emil Jellinek's daughter; he commissioned it, and—as an aside—is entertaining to read about). Unlike what came before it, it looks like a car. It went 37 miles per hour, and crushed racing competition. (Jellinek's previous Daimler swept an 1899 race series going 22 mph.) See Figure 13.2.

Descending, you pass faster and more powerful cars and trucks. By 1928, the Model SS ("Super Sport") had 200 horsepower and a top speed of 118 mph. The 1931 SSKL had 300 horsepower and a top speed of 146 mph. And so on.

However, once you get to the mid-twentieth century, the differential in speed and horsepower becomes less dramatic—a car from 1955 is close enough to one from 1965. Innovations continued and new features were added. On reaching the end, you have seen over 150 vehicles spanning well over 100 years, including some of the oldest automobiles ever built and futuristic research vehicles.

The journey through technology as it pertains to law is not unlike the journey through automobile history at the Mercedes-Benz Museum, only instead of a horse, it might begin with a fountain pen and a copy of Thomas Holley's original legal pad from 1888. The (less visually appealing) journey through dictation machines, typewriters, electric typewriters, fax machines, and computers would bring us to modern technology and AI.

Today, AI is far ahead of the tools Lorie Waisberg (whom we met at the start of the book) could have imagined when he began practicing law more

Mercedes-Rennwagen (40 PS) von 1901.
Mercedes-Benz-Werkfoto.

25074

FIGURE 13.2 The Mercedes 35 HP was a radical early car model designed in 1901 by Wilhelm Maybach and Paul Daimler, for Emil Jellinek.

Source: From Wikimedia Commons

than 50 years ago. The future sneaks up on us with many dramatic changes—some we anticipate, others we do not. We've come very far, but have so much more to learn, to explore, and to develop. In many ways, legal AI itself is, to some degree, still closer to the modernized cart at the start of the Mercedes-Benz Museum, with so much improvement ahead.

A Brief Summation: The Benefits of AI

In this book, we've explored several examples of AI and discussed how it benefits lawyers with several facets of their work. For instance, lawyers can do more accurate work when reviewing contracts or searching for data with AI. Once properly trained to search for concepts, AI should find relevant data or make decisions far more quickly than humans. AI can also help its users handle a significantly higher volume, making it possible to do more work, for example, by examining a much larger set of data. Paradoxically, greater efficiency can lead to more legal jobs.

Adopting AI is a good business decision. For law firms and other legal services providers, it offers opportunities to do better-quality work, increase realization rates, win new business, retain and upsell existing business, and do fixed-fee work more profitably. For companies, it enables them to do work faster and with less effort and—more importantly—better run their businesses, knowing rather than guessing at, for example, the details of their business relationships (as documented in their contracts). AI empowers adopters—through training systems—to create competitive differentiation, build value in the organization rather than its individual lawyers, and potentially make money from capturing and distributing their expertise.

More Automation Is Coming

We have described areas where AI has driven real change in how lawyers work. Much more is coming. Overall, if you are trying to determine if work you do will be automated in the future, a good general rule is that if it feels like something can be automated, it likely will be. Here are factors that make specific lawyer tasks especially ripe for AI:

1. *High volume/high cost.* The more time and money spent on a task, the more reward there is to automating it. eDiscovery, contract analysis, certain expert system tasks, legal research, and legal prediction are all examples.

2. *Status quo limitations.* Some areas of law practice work just fine the way they are done now. Others are done in a suboptimal way because of the limitations of people doing the work. AI can have more impact (and so be more rewarding to build) when it helps create a new standard of what's possible. The status quo of relevancy reviews with hundreds of contract attorneys, reviewing millions of items over months or years, at a cost in the tens of millions, was really bad. Technology assisted review (TAR) software blossomed as eDiscovery document volume mushroomed. Today's contract reviews—often on "samples" of 5–10% of the relevant documents—means that important information gets missed. Many reviews don't happen at all—meaning business decisions get made on a hunch—because human review takes too long. AI is changing that, resetting the status quo.

3. *Highly repetitive.* There is seldom an advantage in taking the time to auto-mate one-off tasks. Repetitive tasks, on the other hand, can be worth the effort to automate them. Software is fantastic at processing large amounts of information with high accuracy when the information has systematic characteristics. This makes it potentially much better than people at many tasks currently done by lawyers, especially junior lawyers.

4. *Fit with existing technology.* The more similar a task is to an already automated task, the cheaper and easier it is to build software to automate it. The cheaper and easier it is to build something, the more likely it is to get built.

AI isn't just about automating junior lawyer work. More experienced lawyers need to pay close attention, too. Ultimately, the most valuable attri-bute of most senior lawyers is their judgment. AI can help senior lawyers make better decisions in less time (sometimes through assisting their juniors to do more, higher-quality work). Senior lawyers who don't take advantage of this change put themselves at a real competitive disadvantage.

In sports, the best athletes have been able to make vastly more money as broadcasts of their playing became popular. In music, the same thing has happened; recording was a boon for elite performers. So too it is likely to be with law. AI should give the best lawyers more opportunity to magnify their success.

AI and the Modern Lawyer

The modern lawyer should be well informed about AI's ability to deliver efficient and accurate legal services to clients. AI is already transforming the practice of law. It holds the promise of freeing many more lawyers from mundane tasks and allowing them to deliver better work.

Lawyers should embrace AI instead of fearing it. AI enables them to do more law, take on greater challenges, dig deeper into the research, save time on mundane tasks, and have the right data in front of them when making key decisions. AI should be part of every lawyer's practice, whether in Biglaw, a small firm, or a corporate legal department. This applies whether the lawyer is in the United States, United Kingdom, Canada, Australia, Germany, Brazil, China, India, or elsewhere.

Say you have gotten to this point in the book and you're still unconvinced that AI is making an impact in law practice now, and don't think it will in the future either. As we write this, it's 2020. Cars are able to drive themselves, computers can beat the best humans at complex games like Go, and solid voice and image recognition as well as translation are available. But your work is different. Are you sure? Are you sure that this will still be true 5, 10, 15 years from now? Technology is almost certainly advancing faster than your skills and the state of the art in your practice area. This change is real, it's here, and more and more is coming. One lawyer superpower tends to be helping clients spot risk. Ignoring AI seems pretty risky, especially when compared to embracing it.

AI is the future of law practice, and that future is now. This can be great for you, if you take advantage. Do it!

Acknowledgments

We are grateful to the many who helped make this book a reality.

Having worked for years as just the two of us, with no or few users, in an area few cared about, we are very confident in saying that it goes a lot better with help. So much of what we have accomplished is due to the help of others.

We have worked with many stellar Kirans over the years, who do much, much more work than we could do alone, and often do it much, much better than we could. They make us smile, and we are lucky to have them as teammates.

Our customers have challenged us to do better, and they have inspired (and sometimes surprised) us with how they have used our AI. We love their problems and their stories, and have become very fond of a number of them as people. Many anecdotes we heard from them over the years made their way into the book. Thank you so much for your support.

Members of the legal innovation community have helped us learn and work through ideas, and often been great companions along the way. Legal tech feels like home to us now; walking a conference floor has become like a gathering of friends. Writing this during the COVID-19 isolation has reinforced how much we value the community. Plus, the community has given us knowledge—or at least some knowledge of who has good knowledge—beyond our narrow area of contract analysis AI, enabling us to write this wider-scope book.

We have benefited over the years from a number of teachers, supervisors, peers, and friends who have pushed our thinking and writing to better levels. While we both have lots of room for improvement, we've come a long way due to this help.

Our families gave us the time and space to work on this project and served as constant discussion partners.

Alex thanks his partner, Winter, who has discussed many of the topics in this book with him for hours and supported him in more ways than he can count.

Noah thanks his wife, Jennifer, who has been a loving companion through his journey in legal technology, and lost lots of time with him as a result of it. It's semi-her-fault for encouraging him to quit Biglaw ;) Her support has given him time to do this book (and help build Kira), and he is very grateful for that. Noah's kids Isaac, Elijah, and Mira have brought him lots of joy. He apologizes for all the time he had to spend on this book instead of playing with them. Sadly, they probably will not enjoy the output nearly as much as his last publication (an illustrated rhyming children's book on machine learning). Noah's father Lorie—beyond being a great dad—talked through ideas in this book for hours and hours and provided important stories for it.

Our contributors enabled us to present a more complete picture of legal AI. Thank you Meredith Williams-Range, Thomas Laubert, Pietro Brambilla, Jörg Hanke, Jack Newton, Carolyn Elefant, Sam Glover, Corinne Geller, Mary O'Carroll, Amar Jain, Mark Ross, Jason Barnwell, Anne McNulty, Eddie Hartman, Dera Nevin, Jake Heller, Laura Safdie, Pablo Arrendo, Alicia Ryan, Amy Monaghan, Michael Mills, Anthony Niblett, and Joshua Walker. Ben O'Halloran, Robert Kuster, Mark Robilotti (and many others we won't specifically call out here; we quoted some in the text) provided helpful background information.

Lorie Waisberg and Jennifer Waisberg reviewed complete drafts of the book, and professors Stephen Gillers and Richard Moorhead reviewed draft ethics material in it. They provided helpful comments, which made the book better (not that we took all; mistakes are our own!). Thank you.

A number of people helped us directly in getting the book off the ground, despite our busy work schedules.

First, the Kirans who helped specifically on this project. John Lute was the MVP of this book. We could not have done it without him managing the process and gently but continually pushing us and our contributors forward. Vinay Nair spurred us to write a book and provided helpful support throughout. David Curle joined our team partway through and was a great help in diving into several areas we covered. Alysha Anzik contributed research. Our (highly valued) teammates Adam Roegiest, Anne McNulty, Corinne Geller, Kennan Samman, Lindsay Smith, Rachel Oullette, Steve Obenski, and Tony Ensinger helped us source stories and explain content. Markus Grupp, Kevin Moran, Edo Cuallo, Linh Trinh, and Joanne Son provided excellent design and graphics support.

Richard Narramore, our executive editor at Wiley, provided exceptionally helpful focus, encouraging us to write a book that people would actually like to read. This mattered. Victoria Anllo, as well as the Wiley editing and production teams also helped get this book done and improved its quality. Rich Mintzer helped us express our thoughts. Kevin Anderson and Mat Miller were able guides through our first time being properly published.

We wouldn't have—and really couldn't have—done this book alone. Thanks again for the help and support.

About the Authors

Noah Waisberg co-founded and is CEO of Kira Systems, a leading legal AI company. Previously, Noah practiced at the law firm Weil, Gotshal & Manges in New York, where he focused on private equity, M&A, and securities. Noah is an expert on contract analysis, legal technology, and artificial intelligence. He has spoken at conferences including SXSW Interactive, ILTACON, and Legal Geek; and has been named the FT's 2018 Intelligent Business Market Shaper, ILTA's Innovative Thought Leader of the Year, and to the Fastcase 50 list. Noah holds a JD from the NYU School of Law, an AM from Brown University, and a BA with honors from McGill University. He authored what may be the world's first children's book on machine learning, *Robbie the Robot Learns to Read*, 256 rhyming words long.

Dr. Alexander Hudek leads Kira Systems' products, technology, and research. He holds PhD and M.Math degrees in Computer Science from the University of Waterloo, and a BSc from the University of Toronto in Physics and Computer Science. Prior to co-founding Kira Systems, his research work in the field of bioinformatics advanced techniques to find similarities between DNA sequences and contributed to the sequencing of the human genome as part of the human genome project.

Index

Let's stay on this journey together.

Visit **AIForLawyersBook.com** for free resources including:

- ✓ AI Maturity Assessment Tools
- ✓ Interviews with the Authors and Contributors
- ✓ Recommended Reading Lists
- ✓ AI For Lawyers Community Newsletter